TOUCHING HEAVEN

TOUCHING HEAVEN

*A Cardiologist's Encounters with Death
and Living Proof of an Afterlife*

DR. CHAUNCEY CRANDALL

WITH KRIS BEARSS

New York Boston Nashville

Please see page 209 for an extension of this copyright page.

Any emphases within scriptural quotes are the author's.

FaithWords
Hachette Book Group
1290 Avenue of the Americas
New York, NY 10104

www.faithwords.com

Printed in the United States of America

RRD-C

First Edition: September 2015

10 9 8 7 6 5 4 3 2 1

FaithWords is a division of Hachette Book Group, Inc.
The FaithWords name and logo are trademarks of Hachette Book Group, Inc.

The Hachette Speakers Bureau provides a wide range of authors for speaking events. To find out more, go to www.hachettespeakersbureau.com or call (866) 376-6591.

The publisher is not responsible for websites (or their content) that are not owned by the publisher.

Library of Congress Cataloging-in-Publication Data
Crandall, Chauncey W.
  Touching heaven : a cardiologist's encounters with death and living proof of an afterlife / Dr. Chauncey Crandall, with Kris Bearss. -- First [edition].
    pages cm
  Includes bibliographical references.
  ISBN 978-1-4555-6278-7 (hardcover) -- ISBN 978-1-4789-5958-8 (audio cd) -- ISBN 978-1-4789-5959-5 (audio download) -- ISBN 978-1-4555-6276-3 (ebook) 1. Heaven--Christianity. 2. Future life--Christianity. 3. Near-death experiences--Religious aspects--Christianity. I. Title.
  BT848.C73 2015
  236'.2--dc23
                          2015023334

*To my wife, Deborah, my sons, Christian and Chad,
and "my tribe," the patients the Lord has entrusted to my care.
Also, to the many great men and women of God
who fed me spiritual food and taught me about
the kingdom of God.*

"We know the truth, not only by reason, but also by the heart."

Blaise Pascal

CONTENTS

TOUCHING HEAVEN

INTRODUCTION
ENCOUNTERING HEAVEN

MY FIRST ENCOUNTER with the reality of heaven wasn't anything like what you've read in the books about near-death experiences. In fact, I was very much alive and well—an energetic nineteen-year-old working as an orderly at a noted community hospital in northern Virginia prior to medical school.

Because this facility was just across the state line from Washington, DC, its patients routinely included politicians, academics, government officials, and military personnel. I was happy to carry out my daily tasks of drawing blood, pushing wheelchairs, and cleaning rooms, but I also got to do rounds with the doctors and nurses there, which is where I first became acquainted with Karl. He was in his late sixties and had been in the Allied forces during World War II. In our hospital—where he'd been a patient for nearly a month—he was still fighting a war, but against a different enemy: bladder cancer.

When I met him, he was full of life. And judging by his kindness and his many interesting stories, I knew he was a good man who had lived well; I couldn't help but be drawn to him. What I didn't know was that Karl was dying.

I frequently stopped by his room so I could hear his wartime tales and take in his wisdom. Meanwhile, I was trying to decide which field of medicine to go into. Desiring to gain exposure to other areas, I one day told the head of the pathology lab, "I want to observe you the next time you're working up a case."

The call came one beautiful Saturday morning. I left Fairfax's sunshine and clear skies behind and headed for the lab, which was housed in the basement of the hospital. After scrubbing in and donning the medical exam apparel, I pushed open the metal doors, and there on a metal table in that cold, gray room was a corpse—its chest open and arms stretched out as if on a crucifix. My senses were charged and raw. This was a side of medicine, a side of human experience, I'd been shielded from till now.

As I approached the exam table, I saw the lifeless face belonging to that human shell...and instantly nausea grabbed me.

"What's wrong?" asked the pathologist.

"I know this man," I said, trembling. "I have to go."

I hurried out of the room, the unmistakable smell of death following my every step, my thoughts running wild.

I flashed back to my conversations with Karl. He had been alive the last time I'd seen him just a few days ago—heart pumping, veins plumped with life-giving blood, sitting up, breathing, talking. In our times together he'd recounted stories of battlefield courage and foxhole fears. He'd been a gentle warrior and a family man. A good man. And now, the way I saw it, he was not only dead but empty of everything that had been *him*.

The naïve kid who had walked into that postmortem examining room was suddenly eye-to-eye with a question that demanded an answer. The words collided in my mind and tumbled out of my mouth in a desperate, angry cry. "Is *this* all there is?"

I stood in that basement hallway, my heart throbbing, my emotions on overload, my stomach nauseated. The seeming futility and finality of everything we do in this life covered me like a fog. In that Saturday-morning moment, all I could think of was my gentle friend—once an awarded soldier with a loving family, now reduced to a lifeless cavity on a metal gurney in a room the sun never sees. Death seemed so decisive, so horrific and wicked—and it terrified me.

I decided I never wanted to attend an autopsy again.

I also decided I hated death and would devote myself to fighting it with everything I could muster. Perhaps that's why I became a cardiologist: a healthy heart is the opposite of death; a healthy heart means there's hope. As long as you have a pulse, you aren't in cold storage awaiting autopsy. As long as there's no flatline on your electrocardiogram, you haven't arrived at your final resting place.

My medical resolve to prevent death and promote health, however, couldn't deliver me from the reality that I was presented with in that defining moment in the pathology lab. This was not a physical question but a metaphysical one—a spiritual concern that had everything to do with the condition of my heart of hearts: I had to decide whether or not there was more to life than *this* life. Whether there is a heavenly realm and existence beyond this one, and what that might mean for my time on earth if it's true.

It's a decision we all make.

I found evidences of the answer while treating patients at home in the United States, and while ministering in the spiritual battlefields of Third World countries abroad. While sitting by the bedsides of the dying, and while standing over those who were once as good as dead—and yet still live. I even saw proofs of this life when I lost my own son.

The answer changed how I practice medicine, and it would change *me*.

These are the stories that helped me realize the heart—and the reality—of heaven.

EVIDENCE REQUIRED

WITHIN A YEAR of that autopsy awakening, I became a Christian. And shortly after that, I started medical school. However, my newfound faith didn't eliminate my need for hard evidence about the afterlife and whether this life is all there is.

As a medical doctor-in-training, I was taught to interpret reality in strictly physical terms. Yet by the time one of my twin sons became terminally ill, I'd seen enough to be convinced of a greater reality than the one we see with our eyes alone. My experiences in medicine—a professional career that now spans four decades—have only served to verify this conclusion.

Till now, I have kept these evidences mostly to myself; after all, I'm a doctor, not a chaplain. But I've had so many views of what lies past the veil of ordinary life that I am compelled to share them.

I know others have done this already in some fashion, reporting their personalized accounts of what happens after we die. What's different about me is that I see evidences of the next realm all the time, in my work and ministry; every day, this life gives us glimpses of the next. These snapshots—from my patients' bedsides and my personal experiences—are what I want to share with you.

I have seen the dead come to life. Literally.

I have heard the tales that dead men and women tell once they've returned from the brink.

I have witnessed astonishing healings and impossible recoveries.

I have been in that sacred moment, even with my own son, when a life passes from this world into the next. (One nurse said it well: "Sometimes you can feel a person's spirit leave the room.")

I have witnessed the peaceful passing of those who were confident of heaven, as well as the sometimes-fearful transition of those who scoffed at it.

As for me, I don't question its existence anymore. After everything I've seen, heaven is more tangible to me than ever. This is significant, because when your senses have been bombarded with the details of human suffering like mine have—when you've perpetually witnessed the assault of disease on the human body—it produces legitimate doubts. Karl's autopsy certainly blindsided me with desperate questions. But what I didn't understand back then is what happens when, alongside that daily dose of suffering, you are given a regular, firsthand view of heaven... and of a God who loves and longs to heal us.

That injection of eternity into the here-and-now can produce life-altering hope despite sometimes-agonizing circumstances. It's what the Bible calls "the peace... which transcends all understanding" (Phil. 4:7). This is another evidence of heaven that I can't ignore.

There are others, such as the medical results and personal transformations I've witnessed that can only be attributed to the miraculous. Through it all, a steady trust has been instilled in me, and more than ever, I picture this world as a sort of pre-op room where we are prepared for the real healing to come. Scripture promises that Jesus has readied a place for those who call on His name. When the veil of this life is pulled back long enough for us to see what awaits, these revelations can open our eyes and transform our choices, making life new. They certainly did that for me.

As I've gotten beyond the walls of the hospital and traveled the globe, I've witnessed the physical realm intersecting with the spiritual realm in even more dramatic ways. The two worlds overlap all the time, but when we're in familiar surroundings, we often don't see it. Both realms are real, just as surely as God is real. And because of these realities, I now know that life doesn't end here.

This is a journey that I first had to make intellectually as a scientist, but then very intimately as a man and a father. It is a journey you will have to make as well. My desire is that this book will help you draw the right conclusion—because it really is a matter of life and death.

I'll be the first to admit: there are many things on the other side of the veil that will remain a mystery until we step through it. God's ways and thoughts are so far beyond ours that I don't pretend to have all the answers. Still, the clues do keep adding up, not just in my experiences but in His Word—all working together to reject the lies of evil, refute our misconceptions about God and heaven, and reinforce the promises of eternal life for those who choose it.

The surer we are of God and the realities beyond this realm, the better we can join in the battle, seeking to relieve the suffering of the sick as well as the suffering of sin-sick souls. Because of the hope of eternity, every son or daughter of God can speak light into the darkness and life into death—it's not just for me to do as a physician. And because heaven exists and God is real, we have full authority to proclaim Jesus as Lord and King. Not just someday, upon our arrival in heaven, but presently, in this life too.

When Jesus prayed, "Father in heaven... Your kingdom come. Your will be done on earth as it is in heaven" (Matt. 6:9–10 NKJV), He wasn't giving us a sweet sentiment with which to soothe ourselves; I believe it was a battle cry to all who would call Him Lord and Savior. We are to go to war on this earth with this truth on our lips: we can have hope because heaven *is*.

Now let me show you what convinced me...

PART I

PROOFS OF LIFE

CHAPTER I

MORE THAN MEETS THE EYE

"Why did you bring me back?" Gary's dark eyes were wide and desperate, his unshaven face an angry red.

You would think I'd have some advantage over a recovering surgical patient in a hospital gown, but I couldn't move—this burly ex–Vietnam veteran had hoisted me by the collar onto my tiptoes there in the hospital hallway, rushing out of his room like a giant out of the forest when he saw me walk by.

Moments like these made me wonder what had ever motivated me to become a doctor. Yet I grew up convinced that medicine was my future. Not only because I was naturally curious and had a heart to help people, but because I was always inclined toward science and its rationalism. Right now, though, no amount of reasoning could save me if this gang leader and his six feet, five inches' worth of full-body tattoos wanted to shove me through the wall.

"Why did you bring me back?" he yelled.

I was so dazed, I could only mutter, "What do you mean?"

He glared at me for a few seconds and then said emphatically, "I was fine where I was! I was okay!"

As he relaxed his grip and set me down, I asked again, "What do you mean?"

All I knew was that just days before, Gary, who was only in his mid-forties and a likely victim of Agent Orange, had been wheeled into the operating theater at Hunter Holmes McGuire VA Medical Center in Richmond, Virginia, to have an arterial PTCA balloon inserted in his diseased heart. First we had installed a heart catheter. Then, as the senior surgeon was carefully putting in the balloon to open Gary's blockage, our patient suddenly went into full cardiac arrest right there on the table. We prepared to shock him once with the defibrillator paddles, but the machine was dead. We quickly recharged it and tried again... and nothing. After a third attempt, we were sure the defibrillator wasn't working, so we started an air bag and full CPR to keep him alive until we could find another solution.

In those frantic minutes, the number of medical personnel doubled in that small room as additional staff hurried in to help. A patient emergency always demands a controlled sort of chaos among the medical team, but on this day, the scene was more chaotic than usual: while a group of doctors and nurses tended to the patient, some of the staff desperately tried different electrical outlets around the room to see if they could get the defibrillator to work. When they couldn't, they rushed to the radiology department to get a replacement machine. Meanwhile, the EKG leads came off Gary's body, and at one point, somebody tripped over his IV line, and I had to crawl under the operating table to reconnect it. Quickly, a new defibrillator was brought in, and when we placed the paddles on his chest and shocked him, Gary's normal sinus rhythm was restored.

Usually, living to see another day would be a cause for celebration, not confrontation. But when Gary told me what he'd experienced during that time in the surgical theater, I began to understand his aggressive reaction. He stated, "I was out of my body and looking down. I saw you underneath the table..." And he added that despite the chaos in that room, he had been perfectly at peace. A peace he didn't want to leave. He seemed almost anguished to have been brought back into this world out of the sublime serenity of those few critical minutes when his life was in the balance.

I might have dismissed his experience as "he's seen one too many near-death reports on TV," except that, without any comment from me, Gary went on to describe in detail what we had done to save him, right down to the emergency exchange of equipment—an exchange that had never before occurred in any medical trauma I had been involved with. And for him to have known I crawled under the table . . . He couldn't possibly recount all these things with such accuracy unless he actually saw them somehow.

I was stunned.

This happened in the final year of my cardiology fellowship, and I didn't know what to make of it. Was this a God-moment to reveal to the doctor that there could actually be peace on the other side after all the hardness and difficulty life had directed at this man? Was I glimpsing the calm of heaven amid the complexities of life? In spite of my knowledge and training, I had no answers. Only questions.

SCIENCE OR FAITH?

My career journey has included three years of research in cardiovascular surgery at the Yale School of Medicine, and cardiology fellowships at New York City's Beth Israel and Mt. Sinai Hospitals as well as the Medical College of Virginia. Now I am on staff at three hospitals in West Palm Beach, Florida. But it took a while for me to get as serious about my education as I was about other pursuits.

Once I got more intent on my education, I signed on for pre-med and anthropology studies at Virginia Commonwealth University—all while working odd jobs and dating my high-school sweetheart, Deborah. I enjoyed my classes and managed a respectable *B*+ average. In preparation for medical school, I took additional courses at both Georgetown and George Washington Universities. I then signed on as an anatomy lab assistant at GW in the hope that having a job within the medical field would give me an inside track to achieving my dream.

I could hardly have chosen more distasteful work—and my intermittent bouts of nausea confirmed it. For that entire year, I was surrounded by death. Literally. And the smell of formaldehyde was always with me, even at meals away from the hospital. I couldn't eat certain foods because they reminded me of the lab.

My job was to work alongside the professors and prepare anatomical specimens for the med students to dissect, and then to clean up after their work was finished. This meant not only handling human cadavers and the anatomical donations that GW received from morgues and medical facilities but thoroughly washing and disinfecting the room and the medical instruments. I was also tasked with constructing the specimens for the medical school's anatomical museum. I'd section and expose different body parts for teaching and install these in Plexiglas cases where the students could view a completed dissection alongside their textbooks.

One day my boss, a world-renowned anatomist, called down and asked me to process a delivery from another hospital in DC. When I arrived in the lab, a half dozen white five-gallon buckets were waiting for me to empty and stage their contents for an upcoming class. Given that we were a gross anatomy lab—studying the human body at a macroscopic level—I expected external body parts of some kind in these containers.

I was completely unprepared for what I saw.

Upon removing the first lid, my eyes registered a jumble of undersized arms and legs. As I removed more lids, my blood pressure rose. These were *not* amputated limbs!

There were probably a hundred discarded fetuses in all, many of them full-term and perfectly formed, looking as if they were sleeping. I knew this meant they were not the result of miscarriages. I had to hold my breath as I completed the horrifying task of lining them up on a long, stainless steel tray and arranging them according to size and gestational age. When I asked my boss if there was some mistake, he assured me that this was a typical delivery from the local women's hospital, and these "specimens" were needed for the next embryology class. I just kept thinking, *These are bucketfuls of* babies!... *They shouldn't be here! I ought to be snuggling them in my arms, not pulling them from a pile!*

Such images were hard to escape, and even harder for me to reconcile. Most of the time, the currents of science comfortably and naturally tugged me along, and I felt completely in my element. But then I would have these appalling encounters with things I couldn't explain or resolve—things that would so drown my senses, I couldn't catch my breath to save myself. Such exposures to the darker side of medicine—and the results of human choice—always felt like riptides propelling me into deep and frightening waters. Try as I might, I couldn't just intellectualize dead babies being tossed away like trash...or the sight of my friend Karl being left empty on an autopsy table.

As I learned more about the complexities of the human body, neither could I comfortably accept the popular rationale that something so precise and intricate could just happen in an explosion of primordial molecules. To me, the magnificent sameness from one person to the next—the delicate balance of chemistry and biology and psychology and anatomy that sustains every human life—belies an undeniable order that eliminates coincidence and shouts of creative genius. Still, so early in my professional career, I tried my scientific best to neutralize the impact and implications of the unfathomable, because it seemed to me this was the way a doctor must think to succeed.

Back then, I believed I had to choose one path or the other—either science or faith; the two couldn't possibly coexist. And since my training was in medicine, the choice seemed straightforward. Yet whenever I ventured exclusively down the path of science to supply my conclusions for all of life's questions, I would run into another roadblock.

Gary.

Or Karl.

Or discarded babies.

Roadblocks that I couldn't deconstruct or detour around with just my intellect.

And the more I practiced medicine, the more I witnessed outcomes that had no clinical explanation—like medically impossible healings or the corroborated details of patients like Gary describing their out-of-body experiences. I've learned since then that doctors often tuck away such events in their mental physician's bag and see if they ever happen again. *Maybe a similar situation will present itself*, we think—and with that new presentation, we hope more medical answers will come.

The thing that still haunted me, though, was the starkness of death. How could there be a lifetime of order and then, suddenly, a fatal moment of disorder—with none of a person's physical functions working any longer? How could you be alive one minute . . . and the next you're not? It seemed to me that order was the true nature of things, and there had to be a return to it somehow after we pass, or else the careful balance of systems within our physical world is pointless. And if such meticulousness underlies our days on this earth, then there has to be a purpose not only in *this* life but *after* this life too. At least, that's what I was concluding as my medical horizons broadened.

A REALM BEYOND OUR SENSES

I was still raw, but my wife, Deborah, whom I'd married in 1978, could tell my eyes were opening to a larger understanding. She had become convinced through her study of the Bible and her experiences with prayer, but I was a scientist first. I had to be shown evidence of heaven—and lots of it—before I could buy in beyond the basic faith of my childhood.

Ironically, it was science itself that persuaded me. Or rather, the limits of science.

Science could only account for so much of what I was witnessing firsthand; all the rest of my patients' experiences spoke to an even greater reality: a realm beyond our physical senses.

I noticed that the dying constantly spoke of it. There was the Jewish man in intensive care who, just before he passed, kept repeating, "The temple is almost ready. The temple is almost ready." So do those who have nearly died. One lady I know reported streets of gold so bright she couldn't look at them, lined with flowers so vivid she couldn't describe them. She could see stately homes in the distance, and one of her family members told her, "One of these is for you." But as she began walking down the golden streets, she heard the Lord say, "It's time for you to go back."

Now she has no fear of dying.

When a person transforms from fear to peace after a moment like that, it is hard to reason it away.

There were additional signs of this other reality. When my own son was dying, there was a white mist in his room that disappeared once he'd taken his final breath, and Deb and I weren't the only ones who saw it. (Since then, I and others have seen that same mist in the rooms of two other believers on their deathbeds.) I also observed that when people are dying, they either register frightful reactions, including shock, torment, or despair . . . or they reveal peaceful reactions such as calm and restfulness. There is almost never a middle ground— it is one extreme or the other, regardless of their symptoms or medication.

Additionally, in talking to missionaries and doctors serving in Third World countries, they would tell story after story of dramatic experiences with so many eyewitnesses that the outcomes were impossible to dispute. The consistency of their independent stories, coupled with my patients' firsthand accounts and my own experiences, confirmed to me as a scientist that there is a greater and more enduring realm after our natural one—a *supe*rnatural realm, where forces of both darkness and light are at work.

I will talk more about those specific forces in a future chapter, but what I initially came to understand was that when this supernatural, spiritual kingdom drops into our earthly one, the atmosphere in a room changes and our physical world—sometimes our physical self—is altered. If the kingdom of darkness is present, there is chaos, agony, confusion, disruption. If the kingdom of light is present, there is peace and certainty no matter how dire the circumstances.

When Jesus was on this earth, He spoke often of this supernatural realm, and He went to great lengths to inform us of the nature of the kingdom of light in particular. When He spoke of it in parables, it was in terms such as these:

"The kingdom of heaven is like...

- seed...planted in [a man's] field" (Matt. 13:24, 31).
- yeast that a woman...mixed into about sixty pounds of flour until it worked all through the dough" (Matt. 13:33).
- treasure hidden in a field" (Matt. 13:44).
- a merchant looking for fine pearls" (Matt. 13:45).
- a net that was let down into the lake and caught all kinds of fish" (Matt. 13:47).
- a king who wanted to settle accounts with his servants" (Matt. 18:23).
- a landowner who went out early in the morning to hire workers for his vineyard" (Matt. 20:1).
- a king who prepared a wedding banquet for his son" (Matt. 22:2).
- ten virgins who took their lamps and went out to meet the bridegroom" (Matt. 25:1).

And when He communicated more directly about its characteristics, He said it is a place...

- where we can store up and enjoy eternal treasures—the kinds of things that moths and rodents (and cancer) can't destroy and that thieves (and heart attacks) cannot steal (Matt. 6:19–20).
- where the least on earth—the young, the poor, the meek, the broken and neglected—are exalted and cared for (Matt. 11:11; 18:4, 10, 14).
- where feasting and celebration are continuous (Matt. 8:11).
- where the rich are seldom found—not because heaven has anything against wealth but because the wealthy in this world are often so devoted to their material treasures that they ignore eternal ones (Matt. 19:23–24).

He also readily admitted that the kingdom of heaven houses secrets that only those who are willing to understand can know (Matt. 13:11)—those who have the spiritual eyes to see and the spiritual ears to hear.

For a long time in my life and practice—until my own son contracted leukemia—I saw and heard with mostly earth's eyes and ears, elevating human knowledge and reason above faith and spiritual understanding. But once Chad became sick, it stripped me of my pride and wrecked my reliance on what I thought I knew. And as I began to look at the unexplainable with a more open mind, it was as if a window into heaven also opened and I could suddenly see what had always been invisible before.

At that point, I understood what Jesus meant when He declared, "Unless you change and become like little children, you will never enter the kingdom of heaven" (Matt. 18:3). He wasn't promoting the immaturity of childlike behavior, but rather the unhindered trust of a child's belief. Such trust is a gift, not a reason for condemnation. It should be no surprise, then, that He urged little children to come to Him, "for the kingdom of heaven belongs to such as these" (Matt. 19:14).

But I had to learn all of this with time. And I had to start where we all must start: by first training myself to see with more than my physical eyes. Michelle was among the patients who taught me this.

NOT BY SIGHT

When I first met Michelle, she was twenty years young and in the ICU, hooked up to a ventilator so she could breathe. A pressed sheet covered her body, yet with her light hair and light blue eyes, she looked like an angel.

Only when I pulled the sheet away from her neck did the shocking realities of her physical condition become apparent: she had track marks up and down both arms from injecting drugs with a syringe. And when I reviewed her medical records, the list of problems was long: her body was wracked with infections, and her immune system was compromised by AIDs and hepatitis thanks to a lifelong drug habit. She was a very, very sick girl. So sick that some of my colleagues privately told me, "She's a dead girl."

My exam confirmed it—the tragedy of life was all over this young lady. And my medical training agreed: she was going to die.

But then a Bible verse I'd read many times came to mind—"We live by faith, not by sight" (2 Cor. 5:7)—and in that moment I made a very unscientific but wholly wise decision: *in faith I will not trust what I see but will pray that she lives.* So I gave her the best of medicine and the best of heaven by praying for her daily . . . and three weeks later this "dead girl" was off the ventilator and breathing on her own. Three months later she left the hospital, and in time, she experienced a spiritual transformation that exceeded her physical one.

Here's the key in my mind: The Lord gives us all regular glimpses of the world beyond this one, but are we seeing them with spiritual eyes, or missing them with our physical ones? When we do recognize those moments, how do we respond? Do we receive them as mere curiosities and coincidences, or do they confront us, convince us, clarify for us, change us?

For me, being exposed to evidences of another world forced questions that I really needed to face if I was going to be the best doctor I could be. But confronting these questions also ended up forcing me to draw some conclusions—and these conclusions have made me a better husband and father too.

What is the purpose behind the precision and realities of this physical world? Is there that much power in a life beyond death that a hardened gang member can have a peaceful out-of-body experience? Will I allow that something may be out there—and then explore for myself whether it is good, and full of peace and light and life as others have testified? Or will I keep discounting every display of the unseen?

These were steppingstones on my path to operating in the light of heaven. And when I reached the end of my intellect and expertise, I one day called upon the faith of my childhood and prayed, "God, I need help with this."

What happened was not like being struck by lightning but more like being slowly awakened by the sun. You can't say for sure when the soft light of dawn slips past your sleeping eyelids and gently rouses your brain, but at some point it does, and then you open your eyes—and somehow the dewy darkness has been replaced by the warmth of a new day.

Now though, it wasn't my Presbyterian upbringing persuading me; it was the truth of an eternal presence and power I was only just beginning to recognize. Finally, I was developing eyes to see.

⚜

My ears had heard of you but now my eyes have seen you.

Job 42:5

The mind governed by the flesh is death, but the mind governed by the Spirit is life and peace.

Romans 8:6

You light my lamp; the LORD my God illumines my darkness.

Psalm 18:28 NASB

CHAPTER 2
LOOK TO THE LIGHT

MEDICINE HAS MADE me an expert at "looking." I have been trained to carefully observe what is happening with a person's heart, noting their vital signs and symptoms, and paying close attention to the clues in their medical history and habits. This is how I diagnose and remedy heart problems and heart disease.

Looking is not the same as seeing, however, and when it came to matters of faith, the "seeing" part of my life was where I needed help. I was witnessing miracles; my patients were occasionally sharing near-death experiences. To a great extent, though, these things were happening around me less than in me. In this important way, I wasn't much better than those with darkened hearts whom Paul speaks of in Romans 1: "What may be known about God is plain to them, because God has made it plain." Yet "although they knew God, they neither glorified him as God nor gave thanks to him" (vv. 19, 21).

Plenty of Westerners scoff that God can't be known; He's too remote, too big, too whatever... if He exists at all. But my anthropology studies in med school, along with my time overseas and my medical practice, would show me how innately human it is to look for a being greater than ourselves. On some level, nearly everyone I've ever encountered has some spiritual inclination—from the Kabre tribe I studied in West Africa to Haitian refugees to Colombian youth to children who are only learning to speak.

This struck me early on in my work with trauma cases (such as gunshot wounds, household accidents, car crashes). I observed that the expression my patients most often cry out in their pain—including those who don't profess any faith—is "Jesus." Not "Money!" or "St. Christopher!" or "Voodoo!" but "Jesus!... Jesus!...Jesus!" Their age or country of origin doesn't seem to matter—children do it, the elderly do it, people of every color and background do it.

In these instances, people aren't using Jesus' name as a curse word either. They say it in anguish, as a cry for mercy in the middle of their crisis. It often appears to be their only comfort.

Why that name? I can't say for sure, but maybe it's because something at our core recognizes that He exists, even if we don't make a habit of honoring Him or acknowledging His gifts.

DRAWN IN

For me, the medical evidences of life after death were certainly opening up heaven and showing me God, but I was still in scientific observation mode more often than not. However, the more I looked, the more I saw. And eventually, on a very subtle and sublime level, God started drawing me in.

Getting into medical school and having the opportunity to study and treat the human body for a living was a huge doorway to Him for me. So was marrying Deborah, the girl I'd loved since high school. But there were other entrance points as well.

God surrounds every one of us with His kingdom at every turn—with messages and messengers, signs and gifts—and He has given it all to us so that we would turn our eyes and hearts toward Him. Some people don't notice because they doubt that He cares. Many more, though, are missing daily hints of Him simply because they're not paying attention.

I'm no philosopher, but if there was no heart behind God's

creative handiwork, then this planet on which we live would probably not look anything like it does. Really, why would an ambivalent Creator bother? He could have just tossed us on a barren landscape devoid of color and texture, music and mountains, emotion and language, where the weather never changes, no one interacts, no one is unique, and where nothing we do matters. If there was food, it would all taste the same. And if time existed, every day would be exactly like the one before.

Thankfully, we've been given just the opposite, a galaxy full of wonders and so much more—every one of which is intended to attract us to the Giver of all good gifts.

When I glance around me, I see a universe crafted by an Artist who longs to express who He is and deeply connect with all He has created, but who is particularly focused on the ones He fashioned in His image. If you've missed His hints, reflect on the past twenty-four hours: Did you notice last night's sunset? Did your child wake you up with a hug and a smile? Are you privileged to head to a paying job today? Were you healthy enough to go for a walk this morning, or at least to open your eyes and breathe in a new day? Did you get to enjoy lunch with a friend? Do you have a pet that was eagerly waiting for you when you got home? Will you have running water when you shower tonight?

Or think of life's marvels: Have you ever tasted forgiveness? Ever known the joy of a wedding day? Ever had a reunion with someone you've longed to see again? Have you experienced peace within tragedy, or love where hate was being promoted?

If you have, you've witnessed God at work. You've been touched by His presence. Do you see it, feel it, hear it?

The first four verses of Psalm 19 say: "The heavens declare the glory of God; the skies proclaim the work of his hands...They have no speech, they use no words...Yet their voice goes out into all the earth, their words to the ends of the world." Whether their testimonies are silent like a budding flower or roar like Niagara Falls, they message: *There is a God!*

But these gifts are not just so that we will recognize God as One who exists. They tell us something of who He is—serving as our first introduction to Him.

His every ray of grace warms us from the windows of heaven so that we might know His kindness and character, His tenderness and concern, and trust Him with our very lives. He is One who cares about details and the delicate, not just power and might. Acts 14:17 perhaps sums it up best: "[The living God, who made heaven and earth and sea and everything in them] has not left himself without testimony: He has shown kindness by giving you rain from heaven and crops in their seasons; he provides you with plenty of food and fills your hearts with joy."

Did you notice that last word? *Joy.* What a remarkable touch from heaven! God gives us a steady supply of everyday miracles like this and, occasionally, He sends more extraordinary ones our way. And if we are paying attention, we will see Him in the midst of all of them.

For Deborah and me, an extraordinary display of God's power and love came in a matched set: after years of miscarriage and an ectopic pregnancy that almost took Deborah's life, she finally became pregnant. And nine months later, our twin sons Chad and Christian were born.

Chad was sandy-haired and blue-eyed, like his mother, with a fair complexion and a sprinkle of freckles. As he grew up, we came to know a boy who was kind, reserved yet daring—and who loved to laugh. Christian ended up the taller one, slightly darker and always on the move, like me. He also loved to make his brother laugh. We could count on him to be the first one to take charge and try new things, and he could never sit still. Both boys were athletic and curious, with Chad drawn to the arts and Christian showing a gift for mechanical projects.

The four of us had eleven very blessed years together. Then cancer surfaced in June 2000, when Chad was diagnosed with chronic myelogenous leukemia. God still poured out His gifts on us; they just came in very different packaging.

During Chad's battle with CML, we saw God's character manifested in ways we would've never experienced otherwise—some of which I'll share in upcoming chapters. But one of the most important things that came out of that family battle with cancer was that we all learned not just to look at what God does but to really see who He is. And Deborah and I would both tell you, were we sitting with you today, that even after losing our son so unexpectedly, God is good, and He is faithful, and His peace and mercy endure beyond every sorrow in this life.

Maybe the best way to describe the journey is this: In our first ventures toward God, we look for Him, hoping He is there. As we find Him and store up experiences of Him, we start looking more intently at Him and inch ahead for a closer view. Finally, at some point (often in our most desperate hour) we draw close and look *to* Him—and that is when we really see beyond our circumstances to who He is.

THE BRIDGE TO TRUST

Looking *for* God has its place as a starting point, and looking *at* Him plays a role in developing faith too—we must examine and question what is in our field of vision before we can draw any accurate conclusions about it, and most certainly before we act on it. Yet we cannot stop at step one or step two. They are planks on the bridge from mere belief in God to an energized trust in Him—they don't get us to the other side. We must advance from looking at what is to seeing Who is.

Chad helped teach me this.

One year he had a small but poignant role in the Christmas pageant at the Palm Beach Day School. The students had worked diligently to make the event a success, but they had also kept their roles a secret so the audience would be surprised. When the big day arrived, the curtain was drawn and suddenly a barefoot Chad in a ragged, sleeveless garment raced across the stage, bowed on one knee, and pointed to a lonely star in the corner of the stage, shouting, "Look at the light!" Then, just as quickly, he rushed off. It was his only line, but it set the stage for everything that came after.

In a lot of ways, that's what his life did for us as a family and for so many who accompanied us through those years of treatments and remissions and hospital stays: Chad pointed us to the Light, and everything in our story with God played out from there. In the end, we saw God as God, and it made all the difference in the face of death and the wickedness of cancer. We no longer just looked at the Light of heaven; we depended on it. And we were forever changed as a result.

This happens whenever any of us finally opens our eyes and sees that the kingdom of heaven is not just around us—*out there*—but already with us. C. S. Lewis, the great Christian apologist, once wrote: "What I like about experience is that it is such an honest thing. You may take any number of wrong turnings; but keep your eyes open and you will not be allowed to go very far before the warning signs appear. You may have deceived yourself, but experience is not trying to deceive you. The universe rings true wherever you fairly test it."[1]

Don't just take my word for it. You can ask a long-ago doubter named Thomas, one of Jesus' original twelve disciples.

Scripture tells us that Thomas was absent from the other disciples when Jesus first appeared to them after His resurrection.

His comrades excitedly told him, "Brother, we have seen the Lord!" But he could only reply, "Unless I observe His wounds myself—unless I see the nail marks in His hands and can touch where the nails were and put my hand into His side—I will not believe this is really the Jesus who was crucified."

Perhaps Thomas had inclinations toward medicine, I don't know, but a week later, Jesus miraculously appeared before His disciples again, even though they were in a locked house. This time, Thomas was with them. Knowing what was in Thomas's heart, Jesus told His questioning disciple, "See My hands? Put your finger here. Reach out your hand and touch My side. Stop your doubting and believe" (see John 20:24–27).

In that moment, says the biblical writer who was there that day, Thomas not only recognized Jesus for who He was but acknowledged Him, exclaiming, "My Lord and my God!"

Jesus replied with these words that would remain true for all who would ever wonder: "Because you have seen me, you have believed; blessed are those who have not seen and yet have believed" (John 20:28–29).

I had so much more to learn about who God is even after Chad died, but I needed to recognize Him first as not just *a* god or the One True God but as *my* Lord and *my* God. This is how I went from just looking to believing.

AN ETERNAL EXCHANGE

God points everyone to Him with the everyday gifts we've talked about, but He also often gives people more personalized signs before they really know Him. These are like deposits in the bank account of their souls—so that one day they may draw out those deposits and exchange them for eternal life with Him. Not everyone takes those markers to heart, not everyone chooses to look to Him in response, but for those who do, He always makes Himself known.

This was AC Stein's experience. When this very wealthy businessman first came to my office for an exam, I asked him about his life and work—as I regularly do with my patients—so I would be able to associate his name and face with some specific stories. As we talked, I learned that he had been an infantryman in the Korean War. During one ground battle, AC was in a trench with other soldiers, and they were being bombarded with artillery fire. Comrade after comrade was dying around him, and suddenly the guy right next to him was shot and killed. AC, terrified that he would be next, recited the only Jewish prayer he could remember from his rare visits to synagogue as a child. When he glanced at the bare tree above him, he told me, "I saw an angel sitting there, and he said, 'AC, you will live. Just stay down in the trench.'" The bombing continued. Grenades were going off, bullets were zinging everywhere, and every man in that ditch was killed except for him.

On AC's subsequent visits to my office, I would recall this story and urge him, "Mr. Stein, the Lord witnessed to you in the battlefield through that angel, and He is real. You need to come to Him."

"Oh, I can't right now," he'd say. There was always some excuse.

Some time later, he was hospitalized and assigned a room upstairs in the private ward. His son asked me to see him because he wasn't doing well. I was eager to visit him, but when I got to the ward, family tension was in the air—not over worries about his condition but over concerns about his estate, and specifically, who would get what. As AC's family heatedly debated among themselves in the waiting area, I walked through the gauntlet into his room, grabbed his hand, and told him, "I'm here to pray with you, Mr. Stein. I know you don't have much time left. Do you remember the angel from the Lord?"

"Yes, I remember."

"We've talked about this in my office before, but God sent that angel to you for a reason. Not just for that moment, but for this one. You need to know Jesus and accept Him as Lord and Savior. Will you receive Him tonight?"

AC leaned toward me with a tear in his eye and said, "Yes, I'd like to do that." So while we prayed together, his family fought, divided. As the kingdom of heaven was dispelling the darkness in his room, his family was just steps away, arguing over the things of this world.

Earthly concerns like wealth and possessions and discord with others can often prevent us from seeing God; it's not just our doubts or busyness. So can pride and selfishness. And sometimes we let addictions or troubles stand in the way as well. But God's desire is always that we look for Him and to Him with our hearts, not just our eyes. And when we do, He promises: He *will* be found.

From one man [God] made all the nations, that they should inhabit the whole earth; and he marked out their appointed times in history and the boundaries of their lands. God did this so that they would seek him and perhaps reach out for him and find him, though he is not far from any one of us.

Acts 17:26–27

You will seek Me and find Me, when you search for Me with all your heart.

Jeremiah 29:13 NKJV

Let the hearts of those who seek the LORD rejoice. Look to the LORD and his strength; seek his face always.

1 Chronicles 16:10–11

The next day John [the Baptist] saw Jesus coming toward him, and said, "Behold! The Lamb of God who takes away the sin of the world!"

John 1:29 NKJV

CHAPTER 3
LOSING MY RELIGION

THIS MUCH I had learned: God *does* reveal Himself, and He *will* reveal Himself to anyone who genuinely seeks Him.

Our interest in Him matters to Him. So much so that one of the poets in the Bible lets us in on one of heaven's realities: "The LORD looks down from heaven on all mankind to see if there are any who understand, any who seek God" (Ps. 14:2).

I had grasped enough of His truth and character that I asked Him into my heart in the summer between my sophomore and junior year of college. I wish I could point to my vast wisdom and maturity and say, "Yes, I finally, fully understood who God is and concluded that I would follow Him for the rest of my life," but my moment of decision was more like a desperate pass in the closing seconds of a football game. When my anthropology professor took our money and plane tickets and stranded a couple of us students in a brothel of a motel in Togo, West Africa, while he went off to party, I hunkered under a sleeping bag with bombshells of panic going off in my mind and lofted a prayer to heaven, hoping the Lord would hear. It wasn't pretty, but it was sincere. And true to who God is, when I looked to Him in that foxhole moment in my life, I very assuredly felt heaven's peace and presence with me.

Heaven was with me even more than I knew, because later, when Deborah and I compared our timing, we discovered that at the very same moment I was crying out for deliverance, the Lord spoke to her at her parents' home in Washington, DC, and said she should ask Him in faith for whatever was on her heart. So she prayed, "Lord Father, I cry out for Chauncey's soul. Let him be born again in Africa."

Make no mistake: there are no coincidences in the kingdom of heaven. At the same time, God has opted not to dictate our every move. The same Creator who gifted us with a world of options extends free will to us, allowing us to choose whether to actively pursue Him or plateau in our relationship with Him.

Deborah had said yes to Christ only about a year before I did, but she was so passionate about that yes that she was way ahead of me, not only in her spiritual insight and understanding but in her pursuit of God. She was zealously attending Bible studies, poring through the pages of Scripture, praying fervently for others . . . and even more so after we got married. With each passing day, God was making Himself more real to her, His presence an ever-increasing force that was directing her life and expanding her heart. And naturally, when a person is on such a tremendous growth curve, you want your spouse to join you.

I could appreciate her enthusiasm and the difference her faith was making for her, but to me, faith was just one of several separate compartments in my life. Medicine had its place; my family life had another place all its own; and so on. Soon after Chad's diagnosis, I actually told Deborah: "You focus on the spiritual; I'll focus on the medical. Right now I'm having trouble doing both."

Sure, I was overwhelmed at trying to oversee my son's care and be the spiritual leader in this family crisis—what father wouldn't be in that situation? But I really did still think on some level, after many years as a Christian, that the two realms were mostly separate.

Until Chad got sick, I balked at any intimations that I might need or want more of God. I felt confident that my church upbringing and my efforts with the sick were sufficient experience with Him.

I mean, I was constantly on the frontlines of life and death in my work. I now understood that God was there too, helping me in the battle. Wasn't that enough?

I clearly still had a lot to learn. And so He kept pursuing me, personally and professionally.

SOMETHING MISSING

In addition to noticing the frequency with which trauma patients cried out for Jesus, something else left a big impression on me in those early years. While training at Yale, I became very close to a colleague named Hal Kitchings, who came down with an immune disorder that landed him in intensive care. Once he was out of ICU and off the ventilator, able to speak again, I visited him in his hospital room. As we talked, he pointed to the simple cloth-covered chair facing his bed and said to me, "See that? Jesus has been sitting in that chair the entire time I've been in here."

I was rather incredulous, because at that point, Hal wasn't a believer.

"*That* chair?" I asked.

"Yes," Hal affirmed with a peaceful grin.

Things like this really made me think. In Hal's case, here was another scientist—not quickly inclined toward the divine, and certainly not looking for God—and yet he was sure he had seen Jesus Himself! Not only that, Jesus had apparently been present with him continuously for the several days of his illness!

That God would show Himself to, and be on the lips of, people who didn't claim any type of faith pushed me to examine my own relationship with Him. I mean, I'd grown up with God. What's more, I now claimed God and knew I would go to heaven when I died. If you went down the Born-Again Checklist that I was sure God kept close at hand, I was a card-bearing Christian in every regard:

I prayed.

I went to church every Sunday.

I attended Bible studies when I could.

I knew how to find my way around a Bible.

I could even be known to share about God with others once in a while.

Yet I hadn't seen Jesus in person! And, I have to admit, His name wasn't always the first thing on my mind like it was for Deborah. Whether in a moment of crisis or in my everyday life, I was more likely to look to myself and medicine, and see what could be accomplished there first.

Was I missing something?

Turns out I was. I had heart blockage that had to be removed. Only this blockage wasn't a matter of physiology.

GAINING GOD

I've always viewed cardiology as a response to an anatomical problem—an obstruction that prevents the heart muscle from functioning at its best. Religion can be an obstruction of the heart too, preventing us from a true encounter with God or a dedicated pursuit of Him.

Little did I know, I needed a major dose of God (and more specifically, of His Son, Jesus, and the Holy Spirit) to be able to operate at full capacity in my faith. Ironically, it would take losing my religion to gain more of God.

Let me clarify. Though they can look deceptively similar, there is a critical difference between faith in God—which can only come from placing your full trust in Him and His Word—and religion, which puts its trust in human standards and traditions and rituals. Faith can save our souls, the internal part of us that lives on after we die; religion only takes you deeper into self, into performance mode, where you try to attain perfection and divine approval in your own strength and skill.

I wish I'd understood this much sooner. Evangelist Billy Graham has said many times: "Walking into a church doesn't make you a Christian any more than walking into a garage makes you a car."

The classic defender of the Christian faith, C. S. Lewis, knew it all too well.

In Lewis's book *The Screwtape Letters*, a senior demon, Screwtape, mentors a young trainee, Wormwood, in how to trip up Christians. Regarding one new convert in particular, Screwtape advises: "There is no need to despair...All the habits of the patient, both mental and bodily, are still in our favour. One of our great allies at present is the Church itself."[1]

Lewis recognized how prone we are to seek God's favor with our works rather than simply seeking Him with our hearts.

Like a lot of people, I was reared in church and raised on religion. My mother would put on her finest clothes to take my siblings and me to Sunday services each week, proper Protestants that we were. Yet we never talked about God outside those four walls.

I always felt good after being at church, especially because I loved the music so much. As heartily as I sang in the choir, though, I just as completely tuned out the sermons. I was raised *around* God—enough that He didn't make me uncomfortable—but I wasn't engaged with Him. And I had no real relationship or connection with Him as I entered adulthood. Consequently, as I've shared already, when I first got into medicine, I wasn't looking for God, but I was seeing Him and proofs of His heavenly kingdom practically everywhere I turned.

Getting the religion out of me was a critical step in the healthy formation of my faith.

When I first started speaking to audiences at religious services, I thought I had to act "properly"—the way the Presbyterian ministers of my past behaved. Use certain words and avoid others, wear a jacket and tie, prepare eloquent prayers, and make sure everything about the event was premeditated and planned for. But when I really encountered God in His power and might, and experienced the touch of the Holy Spirit, nothing was like it had been anymore. Suddenly, I wasn't driven by *have to*'s and *must*'s and *should be*'s; I was completely taken in by One who loved me with a force beyond explanation and who motivated me to dare things in His name that would never have crossed my mind before.

It was the difference between an arranged marriage and a romance. With the one, you obey the process, hoping the gift will follow; with the other, you follow the flow of an unfolding, organic intimacy that you can't predict, restrict, or prearrange. The inability to calmly command how it goes is both its fear and its joy. But for those who entrust themselves to its movements, this utter connectedness puts everything in a new light.

As I got rid of all the junk that I'd been schooled in—the stuff that really wasn't from God—I relied more and more on God's Spirit and His Word to show me who He was and what my relationship with Him could be. I had to start simply, and start small. So initially I did as some of the everyday people in the gospels did: I got to know Jesus firsthand.

A SIMPLE START

In the first chapter of John's gospel, one statement is repeatedly offered to the curious who crossed Christ's path—and to all who would ever sincerely seek Him. Again and again they are told to "come." Not to observe the Son of God from a distance, but to "come and see," up close and personal.

First, Jesus Himself extended the invitation to two of John the Baptist's disciples who met Him on the road. When they asked, "Where are You staying?" He replied, "Come and see." They took Him up on His offer—spent an entire day visiting with Him—and consequently, they followed Him for the rest of their lives, so powerful was their experience with Him. One of those young men, Andrew, subsequently ran to his brother and brought him to Jesus. "We have found the Messiah," he told him (see vv. 35–42 NKJV).

The next day, Jesus encountered another young man, Philip, and instructed him, "Follow Me." Philip was all in, but he also wanted to introduce his friend Nathanael to Jesus, so he told him, "Come and see. We have found the one Moses and the prophets wrote about." Though Nathanael scoffed at first, as many of us do, meeting Christ changed him, and ultimately Nathanael too confessed, "You are the Son of God!" (see vv. 43–49 NKJV).

Jesus went on to affirm, "You believe because I told you [things about you before we ever even met]. You will see greater things than that... You will see 'heaven open, and the angels of God ascending and descending on' the Son of Man" (vv. 50–51).

We should not be surprised that heaven opens up as we draw closer to Jesus. After all, if we want to know what God is like, Jesus shows us. He was sent as the bridge—the New Living Translation calls Him "the stairway" between heaven and earth (v. 51). He was a direct representation of His Father in heaven, and He now dwells with the Father. Getting to know Him personally through Bible reading and prayer was my introduction to a deeper life with Him and a greater belief in God.

I also needed a wider understanding of what I was reading, backed by real-life experiences. I was hungering, not just for more healings and miracles but for a more constant awareness of God's presence—things that religion's narrow perspective had denied me. That's why I started visiting different churches and talking to any missionary I could find: so I could get a global view of how God is working. As a med student, I never trained in just one setting, because I saw the value of learning from different healthcare systems and regions of the world. This approach also kept me from getting locked into bad teaching. The same was true for my education in faith.

Once Chad got sick, I went running after God, earnestly pursuing Him. Wherever God was, I wanted to be with Him, immersed in the moment, to receive whatever I could. This is how utterly fascinated I was with this Person I was just getting to know.

In visiting various churches and crusades, sometimes only one word or phrase from an entire sermon would stand out. Even so, I would take that spiritual nugget and put it in my faith bucket. In another church or evangelistic service, I might get several golden nuggets. They too would be added to the bucket, and I would return to this reserve of truth whenever I needed it.

As often as I could, I also sat at the feet of great men and women of God, listening to their messages, meeting them when possible, reading their writings, and actually attending their events to watch the Spirit in them at work. I particularly sought out missionaries to learn what they were seeing within the cultures they served and how it aligned with what I was reading in the Bible about God's ability to save the lost, heal the sick, deliver the destitute.

In many ways, it was like the first months of a great romance—only the passion has never gone away. I couldn't get enough of Jesus. I wanted to be in His presence every moment of the day and take in every word He spoke. Instead of friending Him on Facebook and viewing His life on Instagram, I was seeking His face—and finding it—in His Word and my time with Him.

I also sought to go wherever revival was happening, so I could witness the different movements of God worldwide. During those travels, I saw and heard Bible stories come to life. Adults who very obviously had been disabled or diseased for years, suddenly healed by prayer. Children too young to know what was going on, being delivered from obvious disfigurement. Demons being cast out. Evangelists being miraculously protected from enemy attacks.

I even got to participate myself, such as with a man in Nigeria, drooling and disabled by a stroke, brought to a crusade by members of his family because he couldn't bring himself. I prayed for him, and the entire right side of his body was completely healed. He left that crusade whole and walking upright without any help.

Back home in Florida, Deborah and I once visited a tiny country church, and the pastor asked me to help with Communion. They had only a small measure of grape juice and bread—just enough for the twenty or so people who typically attended a service. But that night, nearly fifty people showed up, and as we were preparing to serve Communion, I could tell we were going to be way short of what we needed. In the past, I would have hustled to find a solution, but there was no time. I wasn't that same man anyway, so I just prayed: "Lord, multiply this for all the people who are here," and then I started laying out the bread and pouring the juice.

To my amazement, I was able to replenish the elements again and again. And when Communion was done and all fifty had been served, a small portion remained in the bottle and there was still a partial loaf of bread. It was like the biblical account of the widow who fed Elijah the prophet (1 Kgs. 17:8–15).

Then in Haiti, we had a "feeding the five thousand"–type moment (Matthew 14; Mark 6; Luke 9; John 6). I volunteered with a church and an orphanage that were working together to provide a Christmas meal for local kids. Five hundred youngsters and teens showed up, lining the soccer field from two directions. Only two hundred meals had been prepared, so the director instructed us to give one boxed meal to every three kids. Having encountered Jesus and His wonder-working power as I had already, I prayed over the food instead, asking that it be multiplied.

The kids lined up, and we passed out a box to each child. Boy after girl, girl after boy they came, and we distributed the food— meal by meal. I kept monitoring the stack of boxes behind us and saw the pile growing smaller—and still, some remained. When the last child came through the line, a few meals were left. Every child had received one.

After experiences like these, there was no denying what had happened within me: I came, I saw, I was convinced. I'd gone running after Jesus and collected a bucketful of spiritual riches, and when I returned from one particularly eye-opening ministry trip, I told Deborah, "I've seen and felt God. I know He's real."

Best of all, it stuck. It took hold. I was a changed man. Where my faith had previously moved forward in stops and starts as major God-moments occurred, I was now constantly progressing, fueled by the daily assurance that God is living and active and here with me.

HEAVEN OPENED WIDE

A transforming moment for me was realizing God was far bigger than what I was seeing in any one church. Part of my medical training was in Grenada, and I would feel the presence of God in those primitive African-American churches as chickens walked across the floor. When the people started singing, I could sense something enter the room that was soft and gentle and kind. God was in it; His Spirit was there—and people were rushing to Him with *everything*: their trust, their needs, their hopes and dreams, their gratitude and praise. There was nothing scripted or predictable about the services; there was just an expectancy that God would be found and that He would move according to His will. The people in those churches came to Him, not just hoping He would save and heal and deliver them and their loved ones, but knowing He would.

It was so different from the services Deborah and I attended in DC. Back home, I was hearing about the rules of man; here, I was experiencing the rule of God, where grace and love and compassion are the guiding principles. In the middle of an island, in a bare, open-air hut with no sound system and no coffee bar and no membership rolls, I was witnessing what is real about Him and His realm: He is vast. His diversity is unrestricted. His heart for people is unrestrained. And His kingdom has no end.

As time went on, I thought, *If He is this big in the world, then He can be even bigger in my medical practice*, which opened me up to praying for every patient who would let me (nearly every one of them, as it turns out).

Sinew by sinew, my faith was built up and fortified, until I finally understood something else I'd been missing: my patients may not just be suffering from physical illness; other things could be going on that we medical professionals haven't considered. They may be enduring the consequences of sin, or spiritual bondage, or family history. And if they are, only a transfusion of God can heal them.

But for us to bring a touch of heaven to others, we have to have been touched by it ourselves. You simply can't find heaven without pursuing God.

By sharing my approach, I'm not suggesting that you should leave your church. I'm just saying that if you sense the heart of your faith is being obstructed by religion or legalism or the traditions of your past, then get outside your bubble. Visit other churches and search out other Christians to see what God is up to. And then expect heaven itself to be opened wide to you.

We make a mistake if we assume that the presence and proof and fullness of heaven is found only within the walls of a church or synagogue. Religion lives there—in temples built by human hands—but not the living God. He is so much more ... unlimited in power, full of might and miracles, eager to be known. Go running after Him.

❧

O God, You are my God; I shall seek You earnestly; my soul thirsts for You, my flesh yearns for You, in a dry and weary land where there is no water.

Psalm 63:1 NASB

Without faith it is impossible to please God, because anyone who comes to him must believe that he exists and that he rewards those who earnestly seek him.

Hebrews 11:6

Ask, and it will be given to you; seek, and you will find; knock, and [the door] will be opened to you.

Matthew 7:7 NKJV

CHAPTER 4
IN HEAVEN'S SIGHTS

I SEE EVIDENCES of the next realm all the time. But to me, we are already touching heaven. Or rather, it is touching us. Reaching across the Great Divide to reach us.

One of America's astronauts was a patient of mine during his later years, and Deborah and I once asked him: "While you were in outer space, did you ever think about what lies beyond the universe and whether there has to be a God? Did you see or feel His presence up there?"

"Oh yes, I believe there's a God," he told us. "There was a bright glow in all that darkness. I can't explain it, but it stayed with me the whole time."

It would be several more years before that pioneering hero became a Christian, but I heard a very real truth in his words: the experience of God's presence does indeed stay with us.

I just talked with my colleague Hal again recently—the doctor who saw Jesus sitting in his hospital room during his entire illness—and queried, "Hey, man, do you remember that? Do you remember what you saw?"

"Oh yes, I've never forgotten it," he said.

Sometimes that presence produces gratitude and worship; sometimes it prompts repentance; and sometimes it brings profound,

unspeakable comfort amid horrible circumstances. All are charac-
teristic of heaven and the God who inhabits it.

Frankly, though, I've met people who choose not to cling to
that presence afterward; they run from it, perhaps uncomfortable
at coming too close to a reality they can't explain, or maybe fearful of a holiness too great. But for those who reach out to the
One who has reached toward them, they are not only noticeably
changed in the here and now, but they gain the privilege of living
forever in heaven—God's eternal presence—after they die.

NEVER ALONE

From the Garden of Eden till now, God has seen to it that humanity never has to live apart from His presence. In ancient times,
God typically displayed His presence in the heavens, assuring His
people of His power, His direction, His promises.

- After the Great Flood, God posted the first rainbow in history
  to signal to Noah and every succeeding generation that He
  would never again destroy the earth by rain.
- To affirm that He was constantly with the Israelites on their
  wilderness journey, God hung a pillar of cloud by day and a
  pillar of fire by night that for forty years never failed to guide
  His people where they should go.
- Numerous times throughout Israel's history, the glory of the
  Lord appeared as a fire from heaven or as a magnificent cloud,
  leaving those who viewed it in awe.
- When Jesus was born, the Magi followed His guiding star to
  His manger so they could worship Him.
- From noon until three p.m. on the day that Jesus died, darkness
  overcame Israel, symbolizing that the sacrificial Lamb of God
  had taken on the sins of the world.

These cosmic signs of His presence were important forms of
divine communication back then, but they were also distant. I
could see how they might reinforce the idea that God is far away,

remote, a wholly other Being not to be crossed. And yet, what encourages me is that, even as His people were witnessing His majesty, He constantly drew close with tenderness and care for His loved ones in need.

- He supplied clothing for Adam and Eve in Eden so they would not be ashamed, and He delivered bread (manna) and meat (quail) from heaven for the Israelites in the desert when they feared they would starve.
- He spoke to Joseph in dreams, assuring the unjustly imprisoned youth that he was not forgotten and would one day be foremost among his brothers.
- He delivered a ram as a substitute for Abraham's son, and fulfilled His promise that Isaac's descendants would be as innumerable as grains of sand.
- God very specifically answered the prayers of Abraham's servant to designate His choice for Isaac's wife.
- The angel of the Lord personally called, commissioned, and confirmed a discouraged Gideon to lead Israel into battle against its idolatrous enemies.
- He heard the cries of a barren Hannah and granted her a son who served the Lord with his life.
- God protected David through a strategic, enduring friendship with Saul's son when the king was trying to kill him.
- After a victorious showdown against Queen Jezebel's prophets, Elijah escaped to the desert in fear of his life and prayed that he would die. But an angel of the Lord (which Bible scholars consider a manifestation of God Himself) touched him and fed him, restoring his strength.
- Soon after, the Lord spoke to His prophet in a cave and told him to stand before Him and await His presence. The words of the Bible are very poignant: "Then a great and powerful wind tore the mountains apart and shattered the rocks ... but the LORD was not in the wind. After the wind there was an earthquake, but

the LORD was not in the earthquake. After the earthquake came a fire, but the LORD was not in the fire. And after the fire came a gentle whisper. When Elijah heard it, he pulled his cloak over his face and went out and stood at the mouth of the cave." And in this moment, God spoke to his despondent servant with words of instruction and hope. (1 Kgs. 19:11–18)

- God appeared in the furnace of fire with Shadrach, Meshach, and Abednego and delivered them out of it, untouched.

I could name countless other examples, but the point is: sometimes God indeed comes to us in the fire or the wind, making a grand entrance that leaves multitudes speechless. But more often than not, He chooses to make His presence known privately. Through a whisper. A touch. An illogical peace. A silent vision.

GOD WITH US

In the account of Scripture, one baby's birth in an animal's stall heralded a new era of "God with us." When God the Father sent God the Son to this realm, suddenly heaven was not just touching earth; it was here, in the person and character of Jesus! And when the risen Christ ascended to heaven, God the Father appointed the Holy Spirit as our constant Comforter and Guide on this earth, until Jesus comes again.

Within my own family, God has personally made His presence known so many times, and in so many ways, that we could probably fill a book with these stories alone. Two come to mind right away.

When the boys were young—around nine years old—we took a trip to Oxford, England, to visit a very wealthy family. While driving the family's Volvo after a concert on a dark, two-lane highway, I started to pass a diesel truck that was emitting fumes. What I didn't know was that a sharp turn lay ahead. I couldn't see it, and another car was coming right at us in the opposite lane, with the truck right beside us. I had no room to do anything.

Chad saw what was going on and screamed, "I'm too young to die!"

The next thing we knew, our vehicle was *placed* in front of that truck. There's no other way to describe it. It was as if the hand of heaven—or perhaps guardian angels—picked up that Volvo and delivered it to safety, because there was no human way we got from point A to point B that night.

None of us in the car could speak. The glory of the Lord came down and translated us from one place to the next, like with Philip (Acts 8:39).

One of the most powerfully memorable experiences was when Deborah suffered that ectopic pregnancy just after my clinical rotations at Yale. In an ectopic pregnancy, a fertilized egg attaches and starts to grow incorrectly inside a woman's Fallopian tubes, which compromises the fetus and also endangers the mother's life. Surgery is always required; this is one way that ectopic pregnancies differ from miscarriages.

This situation was particularly devastating for Deborah and me— not just because we had tried for so long to conceive, but because we had actually seen our child on an ultrasound at seven weeks, its tiny hands like mittens.

After Deborah was wheeled into the operating room and anesthetized, the surgeon did exactly what he should do before performing a surgery: he probed the intended incision point with his fingertips. When he pressed on my wife's abdomen, however, the entire surgical team heard what sounded like a gunshot in her belly as her Fallopian tube ruptured. Suddenly, what had been a necessary surgery became a medical crisis. Deborah was hemorrhaging so quickly that her vital signs crashed; the doctors couldn't open her up fast enough.

Even after she was given additional units of blood and getting stabilized, her condition was so dire that one of the residents went home that night and told his wife, "I didn't think she would make it." Yet amid that trauma, heaven appeared in a vision that spoke powerfully to a mother's heart: As Deborah was coming out of surgery, she saw a large, outstretched hand reaching through a cloud with a small baby in its palm. The open hand holding the infant was extended toward her as if to say, "I have your baby, safe and sound." This was all the proof Deborah needed that God had our child in His loving care.

She experienced that presence again many years later—though in a different way—on the night we learned of Chad's diagnosis. I relayed the awful news to her in our bedroom after returning home from a review of our son's lab results at the hospital. My first response had been, "Lord, if You are real, heal my son." Deborah's response was to rush into the bathroom, close the door, and kneel facedown before God, begging that there was some mistake.

After a few moments, the Lord spoke to her: "Chad is going to be okay, but you must get rid of your fear." She wasn't sure what "okay" might mean, but she clearly understood the "fear" portion of that statement, and went out on the back porch steps to pray. Looking up into the late-summer night sky, she pleaded, "God, if those were Your words and not mine, do something—like light up the sky." Instantly, lightning flashed.

Stunned, she said again, "O God, was that You, or is it a night for rain? Do it again, Lord, if that was You." Again, the sky lit up momentarily.

Then she said, "Lord, forgive me if I'm a little slow, but if that was really You, do it one more time." Again, a third flash of lightning raced overhead. And then...no more. Deborah sat there for a long while, yet it never rained a drop that night, and there was no more lightning.

Some people would call that coincidence, but not us. This was just the first of many moments we experienced surrounding Chad's illness that told us: heaven sees; heaven hears; we are not left to fend for ourselves.

SURROUNDED BY REMINDERS

Even before there was a diagnosis, it seems we were being given a foretaste of how much we would need to be reminded of these truths.

Early one morning when he was ten, a worried Chad rushed into our bedroom and asked, "Do I have leukemia?" Believing this might be a fear-based reaction to the news that a young boy in our community had come down with the disease, Deborah replied, "No, Chad, why would you ever think such a thing?"

"Because I was told in a dream last night that I have leukemia."

Deborah assured him that it was just a bad dream and that cancer didn't run in our family. But a few months later, the nightmare of a diagnosis came...Thankfully, so did extra portions of heaven's assurance and peace, right in the middle of our turmoil.

For example, the morning after Deborah and I got word of Chad's condition, we went as a family to meet with one of the doctors in West Palm Beach who would be treating him. We told the boys only that we were going to the doctor for some test results.

While we sat in the waiting room, though, a child without hair walked in, and that was it—Chad jumped up and down and began pleading, "No, please don't tell me I have this!" Christian, seized by a wave of nausea, ran out of the room, only to stop short as he reached the bathroom door. Then he caught his breath and turned back around.

"Are you all right?" we asked.

"Yeah," Christian said. "God just told me Chad is going to be okay."

Deborah and I hadn't uttered a word to the boys about anything that had happened the night before, so we knew the message Christian received was actually heaven seeing—and speaking.

We had another such instance a week later. A friend knocked at our door and handed Deborah a book by Sister Briege McKenna, who had been supernaturally healed of rheumatoid arthritis and given the gift of healing. Sister McKenna was scheduled to visit

Palm Beach Island in a few days and had said she would pray for Chad. Meanwhile, we had arranged to fly to New England to consult with the team at Harvard's Dana-Farber Cancer Institute, because Chad's condition was quickly worsening: not only was he losing muscle tone and weight, but his breathing was compromised and he frequently battled night sweats.

The Sister could only see Chad on the day we were to leave for Boston, so I stayed home to finish preparing for the trip while Deborah drove him to a beautiful house on the ocean to meet her. She took them into the library of this home and tenderly told Chad of her miracle. She also assured him that it's natural to have doubts, but that she would help him by believing for his healing. She then instructed him, "When I pray for you, think of Jesus."

With childlike faith, Chad closed his eyes. So did his mother.

Deborah had no idea what Chad was experiencing; he remained silent during the visit and didn't detail anything about it until I brought it up in Boston. But almost immediately, she saw a flash of light in the corner of the room, followed by a vision of a man standing in front of Chad with his right hand over our eleven-year-old's head. Deborah couldn't see his eyes, but he wore a white gown and a brown belt. As soon as she searched for details of his face, however, the vision dissipated.

When Sister McKenna finished praying, she threw her arms around our son and said, "Chad, you're going to be okay!" Then she added, "Don't stop taking your medicine, whatever you do. And be sure to take Communion once a week to be reminded of Christ's healing work in your body."

Afterward, Deborah and Chad met Christian and me at the airport so we could catch the flight to Boston together. My wife told me privately that she had seen Jesus during Sister McKenna's prayer, and she knew it was Jesus because there was such a presence and peace about Him. I wasn't sure what to think, but on our way to the hotel, when I queried Chad about his visit with the Sister, he seemed willing to talk. Deborah ventured about whether

Chad had seen anything when the woman prayed, and Chad's response was immediate: "Sure I did."

"You did? What did you see?" I interjected, still a bit skeptical. "Give me details."

Chad began, "I had my eyes closed, Dad, but I saw..." Then he described the same vision as his mother's—right down to the brown belt and not being able to make out the features of the man's face.

Deborah, surprised at the matching description, declared, "Chad, I believe we saw Jesus!"

His reply? "Well, sure, Mom; what else did you expect?"

I longed for that kind of faith—confident that *of course* Jesus would show up! I wasn't there yet. In time, though, I would learn to expectantly anticipate heaven coming alongside me and my family when we needed an extra touch. But not before reaching one of my lowest points as a husband and father.

In the fall of 2003, our entire family traveled to Houston's MD Anderson Cancer Center so that Chad could receive a bone marrow transplant—our last resort for treatment, and by far the most serious one. Not too surprisingly, his twin brother was a perfect match as a donor. Yet this wasn't something we had wanted to put either of our boys through.

The medical community widely agreed that a bone marrow transplant was a must because the experimental drug Chad had been on, Gleevec, was no longer working, and he had developed a tumor when his leukemia metastasized. He was looking weaker, losing hearing in one of his ears, and an eye seemed to be affected too. Then, after Chad completed a major course of chemotherapy, we received more bad news: tests showed the cancer was in his spinal fluid. It was either a bone marrow transplant or palliative care, where Chad would only receive treatment for pain until he died. We finally, reluctantly, chose the transplant.

Christian dealt with a lot of joint pain from the necessary round of pre-transplant injections, along with several days of chemical imbalance following the procedure. The shots spurred his body to produce an excessive amount of stem cells, which were then harvested as his blood was cycled, all in preparation to be transfused into his brother.

For weeks after the transplant, Chad was as sick as could be, feeling constantly nauseated. Wanting to do *something* for my son, and knowing our family needed all the healing power we could get, I began scribbling Bible verses on sticky notes and putting them on every bag of IV solution that went into Chad's body. Deborah and I also typed up Scripture verses and taped them behind Chad's bed. Finally, we started laying hands on and praying over every piece of equipment and every bit of medication that was brought into our boy's room.

For the several weeks Chad was in the hospital, nurses would come at regular intervals throughout the day and take his vital signs. Deborah noticed that one of these nurses in particular always eyed the wall beyond the foot of Chad's bed while she did her work, and then would smile to herself. It was a wall with only a whiteboard on it, where the hospital staff posted the day's information (such as the date, who was on duty, the weather forecast)—nothing different from any other patient's room, nothing that should warrant any unusual interest. The woman's behavior struck Deborah as a little odd, but she also knew that caring for sick kids in particular is grueling work, so she just let it go.

One morning, Deborah and I had a tiff that really made me wonder if God had left us to fend for ourselves. I mean, we didn't have a community of believers surrounding us, and we didn't yet have an army of prayer warriors interceding for us—all of that would come later. For now, spending day after day in a hospital room with a sick child, in another state and far from home, was about as isolating as it could be for our family.

I was about to feel even more isolated.

I'd returned to our apartment a few hours earlier to nap, shower, and put on some nice clothes, in case my wife and I might be able to break away for a little breakfast. But as soon as I neared Chad's bedside back at the hospital, Chad started gagging.

Deborah, who'd done all she knew to get his stomach settled, was beside herself. "What is that smell?" she asked.

"It's a new cologne I bought."

"It's too strong!" she admonished. "You are going to make Chad sick. Don't wear it again when you come here!"

Hurt that my well-intended gesture had caused such problems, I left the room with Christian and headed downstairs to eat, but not before stopping off in a bathroom to scrub away the scent. Try as I might, though, I couldn't remove the utter loneliness that shrouded my spirits in that moment.

Once Christian and I got back to the room, the nurse arrived to take Chad's vitals. She took one look at the wall at the foot of Chad's bed and turned and asked, "Where's the prayer?"

My wife and I glanced at each other, confused.

"You didn't write anything on the wall today," she said.

Deborah asked, "Are you talking about those verses we've typed up and taped behind his bed?"

"No," the woman replied. "Every day that I walk into this room, there's a prayer or Bible verse written on that wall. The words bless me so much that I always go home and tell my family, and we nurses talk about it at lunch. Even the cleaning people have mentioned it. It always helps me get through my day."

"We've never written anything on that wall," I countered, still uncertain about what was going on.

"Oh yes, you have." She grinned.

"No, we haven't."

"Each day," she insisted, "the words are different."

Deborah and I both had to fight back the tears. Heaven had been with us all along, reaching down into our darkness and bringing daily comfort to the dozens of hospital staffers who were there with us, caring for our son. It was enough to make this doctor a full-fledged believer.

Incidentally, Christian later took matters into his own hands and wrote, "I am the LORD that healeth thee" (Exod. 15:26 KJV) on the whiteboard. The next time that nurse returned, she saw the handiwork and chuckled, "Who wrote that?"

"It didn't look like that?" Deb asked.

"No, it was the most beautiful handwriting."

The presence of God—this time in the form of His written Word—had been there every day, silently securing and surrounding us.

Our eyes and hearts were open wide after this, and we received more reminders. One time when we were in Houston, Joel Stockstill, a pastor and evangelist friend from Louisiana, visited us and brought with him four men from his church. They all circled around Chad's bed, and Joel would read the Word; then these men of God would pray, praise the Lord—and repeat the process. Suddenly one of the guys started crying, and soon the emotion spread to each of them. The presence of the Lord caused every one of those adult men to cry.

At that point Joel announced, "It is done," and he and his prayer group returned home. Both they—and we as a family—had been gripped by the presence of heaven.

Another time, Larry Stockstill (Joel's father) called while we were at MD Anderson, and we prayed for Chad. When we hung up, the fire alarm went off, and the fire marshals and their men came and stood exactly where I'd stood only minutes before. They were looking up at the ceiling, saying, "Something tripped this alarm," but I knew better. It wasn't "something" . . . but a Someone who was watching over us.

Through experiences like these, Chad's hospital room in lonely Houston became a place where my family and I received a much-needed message—a place where the Living One of heaven reached down in our misery, surrounding us, touching us with the truth that we are ever seen and always heard.

Then the LORD said to Noah, "Go into the ark, you and all your household, for I have seen that you are righteous before me in this generation."

Genesis 7:1 ESV

The priests and Levites stood to bless the people, and God heard them, for their prayer reached heaven, his holy dwelling place.

2 Chronicles 30:27

Whenever your people turned and cried to you again for help, you listened once more from heaven. In your wonderful mercy, you rescued them many times!

Nehemiah 9:28 NLT

You, God, see the trouble of the afflicted; you consider their grief and take it in hand. The victims commit themselves to you; you are the helper of the fatherless.

Psalm 10:14

CHAPTER 5

PRACTICING HEAVEN'S PRESENCE

HAVING A SON diagnosed with leukemia activated my faith like nothing else had—making me vividly aware of the reality and presence of heaven. It accelerated my spiritual growth. And it awakened me to the need to practice what I was learning.

Nowadays, I am known for telling my patients, "I will give you the best of medicine and the best of Jesus." In June 2000, when we learned what Chad was up against, Deborah and I determined that we as parents would seek the best of both realms on his behalf.

For my part, I cut my hours at the hospital so I could immerse myself in the medical advances against leukemia to be able to better oversee Chad's treatment. I also devoted myself to an exhaustive study of Scripture, intent on learning everything it had to say about healing specifically, in an effort to find clues about how God works...and maybe, just maybe, a miracle for my son. I also couldn't get enough of books on the topic by the likes of Reinhard Bonnke, Charles and Frances Hunter, T. L. Osborn, Kenneth Hagin, and E. W. Kenyon.

I felt encouraged by what I read; still, I wanted all that we could get of medicine too. So while I fed on those accounts that God was still at work on behalf of the sick, I was consulting with professional colleagues for their recommendations about cancer facilities and treatments. Perhaps between science and the Spirit of God, Chad would be made well.

From all my "miracle research," I concluded that Chad could be healed, and that prayer was a means to it. My reading also revealed that when a group of believers come together to pray, the results are supernaturally multiplied. It is as if heaven gathers its forces and sends an army to earth: victories are won and ground is gained against the evils of this world.

I consider cancer one of earth's evils. So are sin and death and addiction and crime and injustice . . . the list could go on. The devil uses any and all of these things against humanity, wanting to destroy what God has created. Though Deborah and I had few friends who subscribed to such healing prayer, we were determined to storm the gates of heaven for healing; whether God decided to respond by medical means or miraculous ones, we would trust Him.

My faith in the possibility of a miracle was spurred on as I talked to missionaries from all over the world. Wherever they were—whether they were speaking at a nearby church or were set up in little booths at missionary conferences—I sought them out for a one-on-one and asked them to tell me what they'd seen. The stories were remarkable. Powerful. And inspiring. But when numerous attempts to get Chad approved for a seeming miracle drug failed—what my research was showing to be "the best of medicine" in the battle against leukemia—my hope hit the skids. I needed to learn an important truth: "Faith is not a mental exercise to believe the impossible . . . It is not believing 'something' at all [such as a miracle]. Faith is trust in God. It is personal . . . always about believing [Jesus]."[1]

Like a lot of young Christians, I was prone to pursue an answer to prayer rather than the One who holds life's answers. That was about to change in a big way.

FOR MY SON

One day, Deborah urged me to go hear a missionary who was speaking that night in a town about thirty minutes away. This guy, David Hogan, was a cowboy if ever I saw one; all he needed was a ten-gallon hat to top off his rhinestone shirt and leather boots. But he could preach! Better yet, he believed in miracles and the power of prayer. He'd read about them in Scripture; he'd seen them in his life; and he knew God was active in the world today.

At service's end, he prayed for anyone who wanted it. People were so powerfully touched by the force of God that they fainted. I knew this was a supernatural phenomenon referred to as being "slain in the Spirit." Nevertheless, it alarmed me—enough that I started for the door. At that moment I heard the voice of the Lord say to me: "Stay. This is for your son."

I stayed.

As I sat there, David's boldness impressed me, and I decided I'd have him pray for Chad. *Why not? What do I have to lose?* I could tell his prayers were genuine; this wasn't some scripted show being put on by a slick evangelist with TV cameras running.

Little did I know that once I was in line, some of that supernatural stuff would start happening to me! Weird stuff that I couldn't medically explain, like my legs going weak and shaking almost uncontrollably. When I reached David, I told him, "My son Chad has leukemia, and I don't know of anyone who really believes he can be healed."

David prayed with full confidence in an all-powerful God. And then I felt some of that power firsthand: when he declared, "In the name of Jesus, Chad be healed!" I was instantly forced backward twenty feet, but not by human hands. I wasn't injured at all; in fact, I felt awakened somehow. Weak but awakened. An elderly woman nearby clarified things for me: "Dr. Crandall, you've been touched by the Holy Spirit."

When I recounted it to her, Deborah readily believed this is exactly what happened; there was no doubt in her mind. I failed to reason away the experience either, because something had radically changed for me that night: I now wanted God with all of my being. I was so consumed with Him, so zealously emphatic about pursuing Him, that I later called David and told him, "I need everything God can give me in the fight for my son."

The congregation of the church we began attending didn't look much like us; the folks there weren't dressed up or clean-shaven. In fact, life seemed to have beaten up on most of them. But that didn't matter; they believed and prayed like David Hogan, and they did it week in and week out.

Just days after what turned out to be a very disconcerting visit to Harvard's cancer center, another small church was conducting a healing service, and we attended as a family. One member stood out—an elderly gentleman, the only one in a three-piece suit. *Lord, I want that man to pray for us*, I thought. It turns out that Frank Cathey was a church elder, and he had heard about Chad and been assigned to pray for him.

Chad was restless during the service, apprehensive about the entire situation. After the service, Mr. Cathey took our family to a separate room and told us about his own experience of supernatural healing from a back injury. This encouraged us all. Next, the man laid hands on Chad and began to pray. Instantly, Mr. Cathey felt a surge like electricity run through his arms, while Chad started shaking all over.

As we walked to the car afterward, Chad said, "I felt cold air rush out my fingertips." Back at home, while getting ready for bed, he suddenly started jumping up and down with glee. "I feel so light!" he exclaimed. "I'm not heavy anymore!"

We weren't sure what his heaviness was about, because this was our boy who was so sick, he had recently dropped from ninety-seven to eighty-five pounds. But he explained, "I used to feel like I had a thousand pounds strapped to my back. Now it's gone!"

That night he weighed himself, and he had gained a pound. The next night, he got on the scale and shouted, "I gained another pound!" It was the same scenario the following night. That time, Deb and I looked at the number for ourselves and were amazed—Chad had gained three pounds in the three days since Mr. Cathey's prayer.

This pound-a-day pattern continued for a total of twelve days—and our son got stronger. Within weeks, Chad's health had improved so much that the hospital pathologist reported, "If I didn't know your son, I'd say he's perfectly normal; I don't see any leukemia in his blood cells." Chad still tested positive for the disease, but his weight and muscle tone and color all came back.

Experiences like these were building up my faith, but I still wanted more.

HIS POWER AT WORK

A few months after my Holy Spirit experience, David Hogan and I were on the phone, and I told him about my yearning for more of God. Sensing I needed to be immersed in the movement of the Lord, he invited me to come to eastern Mexico and join in their mission's work for a couple of weeks. It was just what I needed.

I'd read, "Faith comes by hearing, and hearing by the word of God" (Rom. 10:17 NKJV) several times over, but I didn't understand it. "I've never seen anyone who has been healed, Lord," I confessed. "I need to see You at work." And that is exactly what happened on that trip.

During my time with David's team, I met Jesus in a way I never had, and I witnessed outright, immediate miracles for the first time. Further, those men and women of God impressed on me that there is a constant exchange between heaven and earth that includes us in the middle because the Lord established things to work this way. All our giftings and service in His name—our prayers, our compassion toward others, our finances, our training and talents, our relationships—are things that God uses to fulfill His plans on earth.

Finally, I gained some essential understanding on this trip that I have carried with me ever since. Those missionaries—and David's associate Greg Rider, in particular—demonstrated time and again that the healing of a soul matters more than any physical healing, and they proved it with their lives. They were willing to be tossed around in the back of a truck for fourteen hours at a time to get to their "Indians," the people they were ministering to; to be away from their families for days or weeks on end; even to give up their lives if it meant one more person would welcome Christ into their life. They taught me that while miraculous healings get the head-lines, it's better to enjoy heaven for eternity than to only reap its benefits for a season on earth. Jesus said as much: "What good will it be for someone to gain the whole world, yet forfeit their soul?" (Matt. 16:26).

Back in Palm Beach, I shared with Deborah the things that had happened, and we both agreed: God was alive and active, and we would make it through this difficult time by His power, not ours.

FINDING MY INDIANS

My faith had been ignited in one evening and invigorated by my two weeks in Mexico. As much as I now wanted Jesus, however, I was frustrated at how so many people around me didn't.

Palm Beach Island is a scant sixteen miles long—one-third the size of the state of Rhode Island—with a residential pop-ulation of less than 8,500 according to the latest census, yet it is home (at least part of the time) to about 25 percent of America's wealth. Business moguls, celebrities, major me-dia personalities, music artists, bestselling authors, and athletes either get their daily mail here (when they're not traveling the world) or have their second or third homes here. This means that every day at work, I treat people who have absolutely everything by earth's standards. Sadly, I find that most of them are closed to God. Their wealth and social prominence and business stature have subtly undermined their desire for the riches of heaven.

My heart's cry was, "Lord, where are my Indians?" I longed for a "tribe" to minister to, like the missionaries had. A group of souls who thirsted and hungered for God rather than the things of this world. I was at a point where I would even give up medicine and go into full-time ministry if that's what it took.

One morning at the hospital, while in the basement waiting for an elevator, I reprised my prayer once more. Its essence was, "Show me who, what, and where, God. I'll go wherever You ask to find my Indians." As I impatiently hit the Up button for maybe the eighth or ninth time, I heard the voice of the Lord say, "Your Indians are your patients. I've given them to you and you alone. If you don't get them saved and healed, no one else will."

This was big for me! I was supposed to do what I had been prepared my whole life to do—but now with a clear mission in mind. That is when I understood: God puts us in a place and among a people for a purpose. We don't have to go out and secure a tribe for ourselves; He brings the tribe to us, and usually, when we open our eyes, we're already in their midst. Patients, clients, coworkers, fans, peers, neighbors, family, a school, a team—any of these could be *your* Indians.

Armed with the answer to my prayer, I couldn't wait to get started. But how?

My first idea was to adjust my prayers. I'd been broadly and privately interceding for my patients since Chad had become ill. Now, though, I felt the Lord prompting me to start praying for them personally and specifically. And if they would let me, I would do so out loud, when I was with them.

I prayerfully set a goal of one patient a week and trusted the

Lord to show me who that person would be. The first week I kept delaying until, finally, I was meeting with my last patient—a former New York fashionista.

My "ask" was nothing elaborate: "Mrs. Green, would you mind if I prayed for you?"

She instantly agreed, and so I took her hand and asked in Jesus' name that she would be well and be blessed. It was about as bare-bones as you can get.

As soon as I opened my eyes, I realized she was crying. Alarmed, I asked, "Are you okay?"

"Oh, I'm fine," she replied. "It's just that no one has prayed for me for forty years. The hand of God seemed to touch me when you prayed. Thank you so much!"

After a few more experiences like this—where my prayers were welcomed by people I would never have expected—I progressed to praying for one patient a day, and then added on from there. Now, I ask almost every patient if I can pray for them, and you know what? In all these years, only one has ever turned me down! Considering that I see roughly one hundred and fifty patients a week, I'd say that's a tribe's worth!

I'm so thankful to the Lord for providing this opportunity. It allows me to invite the presence of heaven into these people's lives. And what excites me is that, at any moment, they might reach out to heaven themselves and be touched by it—healed now, and perhaps healed for eternity.

LEARNING PRAYER

One of the first patients I prayed for was a man who'd been a caterer within Major League Baseball. He was suffering from heart failure and waiting for a donor heart. If a match became available, he would be flown to Virginia's Hunter Holmes McGuire VA Medical Center, which was operating the heart transplant program for all of America's war veterans.

For three months Earl waited in our hospital, kept alive by extensive life support and constant medication. He was so weak he couldn't lift his head off the pillow.

One day when he was especially depressed and ailing, Earl said, "Doc, I'm never gonna get a heart; I'm gonna die."

Recognizing how much he was suffering, I responded, "Earl, I heard we can pray for the sick. May I pray for you?"

He didn't hesitate.

I had no idea what to say exactly, so I just prayed as I'd heard others do: "In the name of Jesus, Lord, heal Earl's heart!" (Short prayers are Spirit-filled too!)

The next day he was sitting up. A few days later he was able to get out of bed. And eventually he no longer needed a transplant. A heart that had been dead was now alive.

I was well aware it wasn't me or my words that produced those results. It was the power of God, activated by prayer in a way that only He understands.

How do you pray for the sick? You just do it, and let the Holy Spirit lead you.

Like any skill, you get more comfortable with practice. It's something like learning surgery. In medicine I gained a lot from books and practicing dissections in the lab, and by observing and assisting other surgeons. But once I stepped up and took the lead on live patients, actually performing operations with my own two hands, my confidence grew exponentially.

You should absolutely make a practice of reading and studying the Word, sitting under great teachers, and observing how God moves. But when you put that knowledge into action is when you'll see the greatest gain. Simply step out in faith—knowing God is with you—and start doing. Heaven, through the power of the Holy Spirit, will supply the guidance and ability you need, when you need them.

I am happily reminded of this every so often, even after years of practice. Not long ago, a man was brought into the operating room whose pulmonary vein had ruptured. I was called in, and when I saw a fountain of blood gushing from his mouth, my normally collected mind started spinning. In that rare instance, I looked at the patient, then looked at the instruments around me—and my mind went blank! The one lucid thought I had was to back off from the gurney and pray.

To read about this probably takes you a few seconds. In the moment it was much quicker; just an instantaneous, jumbled plea: *I don't know what to do, Lord! What do I do? Please let him live!*

Reentering the crisis, I found myself suddenly being guided surgically, one action at a time. It wasn't me thinking; I was being directed, every movement orchestrated by the mind and hand of heaven. The man's life started to return; his blood pressure came back up; his heart rate normalized...and miraculously, he did indeed live.

Had this brain-spin happened before Chad's illness, I would have resorted to every medical means possible to save this patient, but I doubt it would have occurred to me to step back and utter a cry for help. Thankfully, I had built up enough experience with prayer in other times of confusion that I knew to seek supernatural clarity. And so I asked in faith, and heaven provided.

As a rule, that is how we stop the spinning and chaos in life, not just for ourselves but for others: we call down heaven and take action as the presence of God directs. He wants us bringing the best of us to the situation while seeking His help within the work. Whatever results from that obedience is according to His will and in His control.

CALLED IN

I will talk more about how any believer can operate within this power in coming chapters, but understand this for now: every Christian carries the kingdom of God with them. It doesn't matter what church you attend or what profession you're in, the power and presence of heaven is available, waiting to be called into the circumstances of earth. However much you've been given, still more is available. But you won't obtain it unless you actively pursue it.

My experiences with one beloved patient brought this full-circle for me.

Many years had passed since Frank Cathey's effective prayer of healing for Chad. This man of God was now in his eighties with a heart problem that occasionally needed treatment, and I would see him whenever he had any difficulties.

One weekend, Frank went to the emergency room because he was having a massive heart attack. The ER desk accidentally—and providentially—contacted me instead of the cardiologist on call and proceeded to tell me that a Mr. Cathey was in cardiac arrest. Even though I was off duty, the Holy Spirit was telling me to go in to work. So I went.

We took him into surgery, and as we were working on his coronary artery, Frank's heart flatlined. I stepped back and cried out to God, our team gave him the best of medicine, and his heart came back to life.

After he recovered, I was reflecting on the case and thanking God for restoring our friend to health when a single, reassuring thought came to mind: "I know why You wanted me to come in to work on my day off, Lord. Because if someone else had taken this case, they would not have prayed, and Frank would have died."

I was overwhelmed by gratitude. Here was the first person within our new faith community at that tender time who had prayed for the life of my son, and in turn, the Lord had allowed me to pray for the life of this man. Frank Cathey had briefly become one of my Indians.

That exchange is another of heaven's mysteries: when the people of God seek to honor and obey Him by tending to the needs of others, they get blessed themselves. Serve Him, and you will be served in return. It's the biblical principle of reaping and sowing at its best.

I certainly didn't know what I was doing when I first started to pray for my patients. But as I responded to the Lord's leading, He opened new doors. Deborah says of that time in our lives, when my faith became so impassioned, "It was like God catapulted us out into the world."

Not long after heaven ignited my "medical prayer ministry," evangelists Charles and Frances Hunter asked me to come to their church and share my story with their congregation. I'd never done that before either, but I knew we have to start somewhere, and that seemed as safe a place as any. So I went, and I spoke publicly for the first time.

Now I can see it as clearly as my own two hands: God will use us if we will just start.

You may not understand what you're reading in the Word, but keep studying—and then give the Lord time to reveal it to you. You may not know how to pray or share your faith, but keep practicing—the Lord will teach you. Not only that, He will empower you, for our God is able: "able to do immeasurably more than all we ask or imagine, according to his power that is at work within us" (Eph. 3:20) and "able to bless you abundantly, so that in all things at all times, having all that you need, you will abound in every good work" (2 Cor. 9:8).

❧

"Our God...We do not know what to do, but our eyes are on you."

2 Chronicles 20:12

One day Jesus was praying in a certain place. When he finished, one of his disciples said to him, "Lord, teach us to pray."

Luke 11:1

Then Jesus told his disciples a parable to show them that they should always pray and not give up.

Luke 18:1

Far be it from me that I should sin against the LORD in ceasing to pray for you . . . Only fear the LORD, and serve Him in truth with all your heart.

1 Samuel 12:23–24 NKJV

CHAPTER 6
FIRE FROM HEAVEN

PEOPLE ALWAYS ASK me, "Dr. Crandall, why do you see God all the time?"

For one, I'm in a profession where pain and suffering, life and death, are front and center every single day. But beyond that, my job requires me to constantly rely on Him. Because when the pain of illness becomes severe, loved ones and patients quit asking about treatment options and start asking instead, "Is there a way out?"

If not for the remedy of faith, I'm not sure what I would have to offer them in the face of that difficult question. Chad's illness only made my quest more personal: How could I relieve his suffering, in addition to the suffering of those in my medical care? What were the options besides a pill or a surgical knife?

Truthfully, it's a question that confronts every one of us, no matter who the suffering among us are. I work to relieve physical infirmity, but maybe you encounter disease and distress in a different form: poverty, addiction, abuse, injustice, neglect, violent crime, sexual exploitation. We all have someone—or some group of people—whom God has assigned to our care; someone or some tribe who is also seeking a way out of their misery. Which escape route do you point them to?

By the fall of 2003, heaven's hand had been so evident that I no longer considered human methods to be the only means of treating illness. I had been touched by the fire of God—what I describe as the power and boldness of heaven coming upon a person through the activity of God's Spirit. Now that I was praying for and with my patients and my son, that fire was at work all around me, and I wanted every bit of it in our corner whenever anyone in my circle faced another round of suffering. I was finally experiencing my faith as more than a belief system. It is "always...the instrument of new resources," teaches Reinhard Bonnke. "Christianity is the release of the Holy Spirit into the world. Faith itself is not power, but the link to power."[1]

According to the book of Acts, the believers in Jerusalem right after Jesus' resurrection were touched by that power when the Holy Spirit came upon them on the day of Pentecost. Supernatural tongues of fire came to rest on each one of them, and they began speaking in a host of languages—foreign languages these believers didn't know themselves, but that the Spirit caused them to speak. (This spiritual phenomenon is known as "speaking in tongues.")

This created such a stir among the assembled Jews in Jerusalem that one of Jesus' disciples, Peter, had to put it in perspective for the crowd. A new era was being ushered in, he explained—one that both the prophet Joel and Jesus Himself had foretold. Peter reminded the crowd of what the Lord had said to Joel: "Your sons and daughters will prophesy; your young men will see visions, your old men will dream dreams. Even on my servants, both men and women, I will pour out my Spirit...I will show wonders in the heaven above and signs on the earth below, blood and fire and billows of smoke...before the coming of the great and glorious day of the Lord. And everyone who calls on the name of the Lord will be saved" (Acts 2:16–21, quoting Joel 2:28–32).

The tongues of fire and the world languages being spoken were symbols of the initiation of that prophetic age. The Holy Spirit had been unleashed and would now be constantly present with the people of God, empowering them with boldness and the forces of heaven so that they would be able to perform even greater miracles than Jesus had.

This additional anointing of power and spiritual gifting is exactly what I received in that evangelistic service with David Hogan, and I was eager to take it in greater measure to everyone in my care if I could. That experience also sealed my belief that Chad could be healed by the name of Jesus; the way I understood it, because it is always the will of God to heal, I just needed to expose my son to all the healing prayer he could get.

A natural opportunity came during our prolonged stay at MD Anderson in Houston. I got restless with all the waiting that is part of battling an ongoing illness. We had to wait on test results, treatments to take effect, the right conditions for the next proce-dure... It was all I could tolerate; I wanted everything to be moving forward at all times.

One way to put our wait time to use—and to surround my son with praying Christians—was for our family to volunteer with a ministry, so I contacted Charles and Frances Hunter. I'd never met them, but their book on healing the sick[2] had reassured me that I wasn't crazy to think miracles still happen today.

They welcomed us into their work. While we assembled mail-ings and burned CDs for their ministry distribution (even Chad helped, when he felt up to it!), our entire family was witness to the healing power of heaven. We also gained an army of prayer warriors who would see us through our battle with leukemia and beyond.

The Hunters' team surrounded us with prayer and became spiri-tual family, but so did others we met, like members of Joel Osteen's church and the Stockstills. As word of Chad's condition spread within the faith community, sisters and brothers in the Lord would come wherever we were at the time to lay hands on Chad and ask the Lord for his healing. The support was astounding—and such a change from the isolation we'd felt for so long.

Men and women of God from all over the world met with us and prayed for us. Pastor César Castellanos, the "Billy Graham of

South America," even flew in and out of Florida from Colombia in the same day, simply to pray for Chad in our home.

I had faith that the prayers of these righteous ones were "powerful and effective"—the Bible says as much. It wasn't until some time later, though, that I realized how much spiritual authority was mine.

HEAVEN DESCENDING

I started to get the picture when a missionary friend, Andrew McMillan, invited me to come to Colombia, South America, and minister with him. I first spoke to a group of about two hundred and fifty young men; next, Andrew asked me to present a message to fifteen hundred youth at a gathering in his church. I had intended to shadow him at service's end as he prayed for the Spirit to heal and touch these kids, but while I was exhorting the crowd— "You can have boldness to tell others about Christ if you'll ask for it in Jesus' name"—a greater courage swept over *me*, and I offered to pray for them to receive this gift right then and there.

As soon as I held up my hand and began interceding, those kids started falling down slowly, peacefully, in what I can only describe as the wave of God. It was like a domino effect; one after another they went completely out, unconscious, thoroughly slain in the Spirit. Young people were touched by God's Holy Spirit all over that room.

That same experience has followed Deborah and me ever since. At that moment, though, I was dumbfounded.

Andrew, who had never seen such an all-encompassing movement of the Spirit, asked me to speak and pray at upcoming services. I did, and the same thing happened—only in larger numbers. People were overcome by the Spirit, demons were removed, and the lost were drawn to Christ as we laid hands on and prayed for all those in attendance.

I didn't feel anything unique during these services; in fact, I was abundantly aware that the power of what was happening wasn't within me; it was outside of me and in front of me—almost like a force field. My role was to simply be obedient to whatever the Spirit prompted me to do and say.

As a doctor, I still can't tell you what exactly happens when someone is slain in the Spirit; there is no medical reason for it whatsoever. I even talked to Reinhard Bonnke about it early on because I thought it was weird. Yet wherever we go—wherever the power of God and the Word of God are being preached—people's knees buckle and they fall to the ground. Not chaotically or violently, but gently, almost delicately. Or an overwhelming quietness and peace comes over them. Or they are overcome with tears. Or, as happened with me, they start shaking. One of my neighbor's legs shook for two days straight under the glory of God after accepting Christ.

Often there will be a temperature change in the room as well, accompanied by a sweet, pleasant breeze—the soft wind of the Spirit always seems to me to sweep from the right side of the room to the left. Deborah sees sparkling flickers of light in the heavens whenever the Spirit is moving.

These things don't happen every time, but when similar events occur often enough in vastly different settings, they reassure you that God is present and that these signs are direct from heaven.

I can only explain it as the presence of the Spirit touching people. Sometimes His wave falls when we lay hands on people. Other times, person after person goes down even before they've been touched, just as the praying starts. Afterward, they report feeling an enormous peace and joy; it turns out to be a life-changing blessing.

What I gained from this is the understanding that spiritual touch—physically laying hands on someone—has great power and authority. Nowadays I like to lay hands on my patients' foreheads or shoulders, and often I'll anoint the sick with oil right there in my office, which represents the Holy Spirit touching them. At the point of contact an exchange takes place where the kingdom of heaven is delivered to the one on earth. And when kingdom touches kingdom, things change.

With both my son and my patients, peace would descend, or fear would be removed. Being touched by the Spirit of heaven not only gave me a radical boldness to minister to others, but it empowered me to enthusiastically pursue additional means of helping my patients—spiritual means. As time went on, I cared less and less how people viewed me or reacted to me. It didn't matter whether they considered me a Jesus freak or a crazy doctor; I was willing to put it all out there and do whatever God asked so they would see Him. This gave me great freedom to operate in the Spirit and invite heaven into any and every situation, medical or otherwise.

When I did start using my spiritual authority to call down heaven into the scenes of earth, other believers were strengthened in their faith and nonbelievers were convinced that the God of my prayers was the true and living God. A similar thing happened in Acts with the apostles—their boldness was ignited and they went forth with power to spread the gospel to the ends of the earth.

THE SHOWDOWN

Probably the most epic instance of "calling heaven down" in Scripture was Elijah's confrontation with King Ahab's religious men in 1 Kings 18. Today it would be billed as "The Showdown on Mount Carmel"—the Old Testament equivalent of Super Bowl Sunday.

Elijah the prophet summoned all the people of Israel to meet him on the mountain and challenged King Ahab to send all four hundred and fifty of his prophets of Baal to the site. God's servant then confronted the people of the Lord before it all began: "How long will you waver between two opinions? If the LORD is God, follow him; but if Baal is God, follow him" (v. 21).

He told them to get two bulls and let the prophets of Baal choose theirs, cut it into pieces, and put it on their altar them-selves. Elijah would do the same with the other bull; then each "team" would call on their deity, and the victor would be decisively declared in this way: "The god who answers by fire—he is God" (v. 24).

The prophets started calling on Baal first thing in the morning. They danced and shouted around their altar and beseeched their god, to no avail.

Around noon, Elijah started mocking them: "Shout louder!... Perhaps [your god] is deep in thought, or busy, or traveling. Maybe he is sleeping" (v. 27). So the prophets made more noise and cut themselves until they drew blood, keeping up their efforts until evening. The biblical record is telling here: "But...no one answered, no one paid attention" (v. 29).

Finally, when it was his turn, Elijah repaired the broken-down altar of the Lord, dug a trench around it, cut his bull into pieces and laid it on the wood, and then told the people to douse the sacrifice and the altar with four large vessels of water. They did so, and he had them repeat the dousing two more times. The sacrifice was so saturated that the water ran off the altar and filled the trench. Next, Elijah prayed one simple prayer, calling down the power of heaven into the sphere of earth: "Lord...let it be known that you are God in Israel...Answer me, Lord, so these people will know that you, Lord, are God, and that you are turning their hearts back again" (vv. 36–37).

Scripture reports that the fire of the Lord fell immediately and burned up not only the sacrifice but the wood, the stones of the altar, the water in the trench, and even the soil that the altar sat on! And the people fell on their faces, knowing they had witnessed the living God in action. After this, the Lord ended Israel's long drought and sent rain over the land. Heavenly fire, then healing rain.

WITH AUTHORITY

The more I have invited heaven into the operating and exam room, the more healing power I have seen at work—and the more others have recognized the hand of God.

Recently, our emergency room team treated a very rich elderly man who had suffered a stroke. He couldn't move his right arm or leg, and he had aphasia, meaning he was unable to speak. The team had done everything they could do for him and made sure he was stabilized, but the results of the stroke were pretty severe and they weren't convinced he would improve. Still, his wife asked me, "Will you come pray for him?"

The female doctor in the ER was watching as I did this. "In the name of Jesus, I bind the spirit of death, infirmity, and illness and take authority over you!" I prayed. "Lord Jesus, heal this man!"

The next day, the patient was fully functional—no sign of stroke whatsoever. The doctor remarked, "That is impossible; I examined him yesterday! It must've been your prayer that did it."

Actually, it was my God who did it. And I always want to make sure He gets the glory, because I don't ever enter into the battle for souls or physical healing in my own strength. We have to go in the fullness of the power of heaven in Jesus' name, totally obedient to the Spirit's promptings and with our pride completely surrendered. As we do, God will give us even more power. He always has more for us; the supply never ends for those who obediently pursue Him.

To have the fire of God means more truth is being constantly revealed to you. The power of the Spirit can be an enduring power, just as growth in Christ can be a perpetual growth. It's not only about attending church or daily prayer and Bible reading; we strive after the glory of God so that wherever we go, work, or speak, His dominion is welcomed and free to work.

For every believer (not just me!), the kingdom of God enters every place with you to initiate change and victory, if you will call it down.

I have the authority of medicine *and* the kingdom of God with me whenever I walk into an exam room or approach a hospital bed. Whatever you're good at, you carry with you the authority of your profession or expertise—be it business or education or the creative arts or childrearing. And...if you're a follower of Christ, you can also enter your home or workplace, confident that you have the authority of heaven with you as well. That boldness changes the spiritual atmosphere. It also should change how we as believers approach suffering of any kind.

OPERATING IN THE SPIRIT

I was able to share this with a Christian couple I met this past spring. The woman was developing anxiety, so we discussed some medical support for her, but I also prayed for her. Then I told the husband, "You can do this at home when she starts getting anxious: pray, 'I proclaim peace over my wife in Jesus' mighty name...'"

Operating in the Spirit and summoning heaven into earth's suffering doesn't come naturally at first. But the more you see heaven move, the more you remember to invite it in. My accountant, Jonathan, learned this for himself when he accompanied me on a trip to Haiti back in 2010, after a devastating earthquake ravaged the country.

With its water supply contaminated, the tiny island suffered an outbreak of deadly cholera, and the Haitians needed all the help they could get. So Jonathan and I traveled to Port au Prince to volunteer at a cholera camp for two weeks.

This particular camp was being run by a Catholic children's hospital. They had set up fourteen large white-canvas military tents on their grounds, with fourteen green military cots per tent. These tents had no ventilation, and the temperature inside would sometimes get up to well over one hundred degrees. It was a hellish place for people who were already suffering from the fever and nausea of cholera, yet the hospital just didn't have the resources to house these patients anywhere else.

By the time we arrived, a Hollywood director had been heading up the humanitarian efforts at the camp for two weeks, and he was completely worn out. He met us in the first tent—where the sickest victims were—filled us in on their operations thus far, and turned the supply keys over to me. Among the details he communicated were that three or four people were dying every day, mostly the young or the elderly. The death toll was rising so fast that they kept cardboard coffins piled right outside the tents.

These were just tragic circumstances.

Reality wasn't about to let up for us newcomers either. Lying on the very first cot, as soon as we entered the tent, was the body of a woman who had just died. While the director reviewed what we needed to know about the work, some of the camp aides quietly came over, wrapped the woman in a sheet, and removed her from the tent. It was a troubling scene for me, but for Jonathan, it was downright alarming.

By the time the director left, the accountant in Jonathan had sized up the enormity of the situation, and he whispered to me, "What are you going to do?"

"I'm going to treat these patients and we're going to pray in the name of Jesus!" I replied. "Follow me and pray what I'm praying."

I began, "You spirit of death, the kingdom of God has arrived, and you have no place here. I call the kingdom of God down now in this tent, and I cast you out, you spirit of death, in the mighty name of Jesus!" Then I said to Jonathan, "We're ready. Let's go to the other tents."

We proceeded from one quarantine tent to the next, and while I hooked up IV bags and showed Jonathan and the Haitian aides how to assist the patients medically, I would say out loud, "You spirit of death, in the name of Jesus, the kingdom of God has arrived, and I cast you out!" Jonathan stayed with me, somberly taking it all in and helping where he could.

It took us until late evening to finish seeing all the patients and trying to make them more comfortable. I know our medicine helped them, but something far greater happened: heaven broke in! And it wasn't just because I was trying to be obedient to the Spirit.

In a matter of days, Jonathan too was praying the kingdom of heaven down! He claimed the children's tents as his territory and covered the east end of the camp all by himself, while I made rounds in the adult tents on the west end. He would hold the children, feed them, tend to their fevers, and pray. I could hear him pleading, almost yelling to heaven, "Baby, be healed in Jesus' name!" And you know what? Not only did no children die while we were there, but the sick were actually being healed!

The change throughout the camp was remarkable enough that the hospital administrator, who'd been on site from the very first days after the quake, asked, "Doctor, what did you do? People are getting better instead of dying!"

"We prayed in the name of Jesus," I said.

"Then your God must be real," he replied.

That's what the fire of heaven does: it reaches down and empowers the citizens of earth—healing some, convincing others, making brave the timid.

I used to always wonder: "But what if I don't feel the Holy Spirit with me in a situation?" Well, my spiritual mentors have taught me to pray anyway, knowing Jesus has given us His own authority to cure diseases (Luke 9:1).

Heaven will make itself known when it is time. Our job is to invite it into the battle with us.

Just weeks ago, one of the nurses I work with told me her whole body felt like it was on fire when I started speaking in tongues during a surgery. I had momentarily stepped back at something that surprised me, and a spiritual language spontaneously came out of my mouth. Heaven dropped in during that moment, and she recognized it as much as I did.

There was a time when I thought that calling down heaven's healing and deliverance was for spiritual snake charmers—people who were on the fringe. Now, I've seen its power so often that I'm determined not to deter others. I don't ever want to be guilty of what Jesus condemned the teachers of His day for: "Woe to you ... you hypocrites! You shut the door of the kingdom of heaven in people's faces. You yourselves do not enter, nor will you let those enter who are trying to" (Matt. 23:13).

The door of the kingdom of heaven has been opened to me, and now I'm intent on opening it up to everyone I meet as well. Because through that doorway is the only way out of the pain of this life—a healing power for body, soul, and spirit that is not of this earth.

⸺

Confess your sins to each other and pray for each other so that you may be healed. The prayer of a righteous person is powerful and effective.

James 5:16

He was given authority, glory and sovereign power; all nations and peoples of every language worshiped him. His dominion is an everlasting dominion that will not pass away, and his kingdom is one that will never be destroyed.

Daniel 7:14

Jesus came and told his disciples, "I have been given all authority in heaven and on earth. Therefore, go and make disciples of all the nations, baptizing them in the name of the Father and the Son and the Holy Spirit. Teach these new disciples to obey all the commands I have given you. And be sure of this: I am with you always, even to the end of the age."

Matthew 28:18–20 NLT

CHAPTER 7
TWO KINGDOMS

NOT UNTIL ALL these things happened in my spiritual life did I really consider that there's an entire *realm* beyond what we see. Not just a heaven and a hell, but two kingdoms with armies and spiritual forces—demons and angels.

For many years, I think I lodged the activity of angels and demons in a similar category with speaking in tongues and being slain in the Spirit: that is, only kooks and fanatics put any stock in that stuff. But the little Pentecostal church our family started attending after Chad's diagnosis claimed that it was all true: a war is going on in the heavens; God's angelic army is fighting for souls; and Satan's forces are no joke.

I went so far as to tell the pastor, "Next time you see one of those demons, let me know."

One Sunday the minister took me up on my challenge and beckoned me to come up front. "You want to see a demon?" he asked. "There's one."

From his vantage point I saw a man standing nearby, undulating and hissing like a snake, his eyes rolled back in his head. I knew it wasn't a put-on when I glimpsed who it was: this wasn't some drug addict or mentally ill person; the man was a doctor, just like me. And he was as educated as they come.

That was my first obvious encounter with the underworld.

Then, as I started traveling with evangelists, I saw things like this regularly.

I once flew to hear a missionary from Mexico speak at a farming community in South Dakota. The meeting was in a theater, and as the missionary prayed over the crowd, many people were slain in the Spirit. Some, though, manifested demons. I remember one woman in particular; she started spinning at an impossible speed and growling.

I asked the preacher, "What's going on?" and he replied, "This woman is loaded with demons and we are going to cast them out."

At the name of Jesus she stopped and came to her senses, and afterward, she told us she'd come to the meeting to be delivered.

This was all new territory to me then. Shockingly new. But such instances became part of my training in spiritual warfare. Now I've learned to, if not expect spiritual activity, at least not be surprised by it.

SPIRITUAL BOOT CAMP

Deborah and I both felt that Chad's illness was a spiritual boot camp for us. Thankfully, our family now had fellow believers—the pastors and missionaries and ministry teams and individual Christians we met along the way—who taught us how to fight in the spiritual realm.

We learned not just to recognize physical manifestations of light versus dark but the power that was in the name of Jesus and the blood of His cross. We learned the importance of preparing ourselves like soldiers. Prayer and fasting and immersion in the Scriptures became part of our arsenal. So did all the books on miracles and healing that we could get our hands on. Whatever was happening—whatever approach we took—it had to be backed up by the Word or else it wasn't of God. (That's why it's important to spend time with more mature Christians who have seen more and understand more. They helped train us in the Scriptures and how to use the Word against the enemy, as Jesus did when Satan tempted Him in the wilderness.)

I also gained a lot from talking with patients who had flatlined and then been revived. If they'd had any type of supernatural experience, I found they were eager to talk to somebody about what they saw and heard. Especially someone who was willing to believe them. So I made a habit of visiting with them immediately afterward, while the details were still fresh, and letting them share. Their stories became "case studies" of a sort that I could reflect on and learn from.

Over the years, numerous people have spoken of seeing angels or being ministered to by them—this is fairly frequent. Many have reported feeling surrounded by an otherworldly peace or kindness; some have talked of being drawn toward a light or a tunnel; and a lot of my patients have seen dead family members or friends. They report such instances more often than you would think too, probably in over half the cases. It's also common for people who have had out-of-body experiences to see their surviving loved ones crying or praying in other rooms, and to be able to tell you which rooms, even if they've never been in our hospital before.

Jackson, a friend of our family, was only seventeen or eighteen, his kidneys failing, when he saw angels ascending and descending a staircase, much like Jacob in the Bible did. When I am doing ministry, people commonly report seeing angels around me or around the crowd during the worship portion of the service. And why not? Hebrews 1:14 tells us that angels are "ministering spirits" dispatched by the throne of heaven "to serve those who will inherit salvation."

I've also had patients who spoke of the opposite: they've shared terrifying accounts of being in hell-like surroundings or coming face-to-face with evil beings. One patient of mine, Jeff, just before he experienced a huge miracle that I'll share in the next chapter, reported actually being in hell, fully conscious, his senses completely engaged. He told me he'd been in utter darkness, shelved away in a casket inside a room, and devastated that no one came to visit him—not his ex-wife or daughter, his friends, his coworkers, or his extended family. He kept saying, "I'm so disappointed. So disappointed."

As if that wasn't unnerving enough, two men came in to where he was, wrapped him up, and threw him in the trash. He could not have felt more desolate or abandoned.

That story alone should make skeptics shudder because, in biblical times, the refuse of Jerusalem was taken to a trash pit outside the city—to a valley called Gehenna (or Ben Hinnom, translated "hell" in the New International Version), where waste was burned twenty-four hours a day, every day (Matt. 5:22; 18:9). According to *Nave's Topical Bible*, "Jewish apocalyptic writers called it the entrance to hell, and it became a figure of hell itself. Jesus used the term *gehenna* . . . in this sense."[1]

Jeff didn't know any of this at the time—he was not a believer. So the historical facts give additional credibility to his experience. Still, a lot of people continue to deny that there is a hell or a prince of darkness ruling over the powers of evil. All I can say is: the enemy gains ground whenever people fail to believe he exists.

Between my family's experiences, those of my patients, and the demonic oppression I've seen with my own two eyes, I couldn't be more convinced.

ENCOUNTERS WITH THE DARKNESS

One Muslim man, prior to his conversion to Christianity, would sometimes come to my office to be prayed for, saying, "The dark man is after me. He's back, and he's wanting my life."

On one of our stays in Houston, Chad saw a red lion's head in the corner of the room, and when he began to pray, it left. As soon as Christian heard about this, he got out the anointing oil and made huge floor-to-ceiling crosses all over the windows. The next day you could see their dripped outlines in the sun's reflection.

Another time, during a two-week period in which Chad couldn't sleep, Deborah knelt beside him in the living room to pray, and then suggested that Chad keep praying while she went to get something in another room. He soon came running after her, terrified. "Mom, there were three demons in the corner with their heads back, laughing at me! They were dressed in black, and their heads were like triangles!" When Deborah later visited Lakewood Church in Houston, one of the elders told her his wife had also seen demons wearing black, with triangular, wolflike heads.

I had my own vision of hell within months of Chad's diagnosis. In the dream I was in a three-story barn, and as I struggled to get to the top floor, a door to an inferno busted wide open. The fire seemed intent on pulling me in with the bucket I held in my hand. After a lengthy tug-of-war, I finally released the bucket, and it was snatched into the blazing fire before I made my way back out of the barn.

I can't say for sure what it meant, but I felt it was Satan's attempt to scare me into passivity and away from pursuing all that the Holy Spirit had for me.

None of this activity should really be a surprise. After all, Jesus and His disciples regularly encountered and delivered the demon-possessed in their day—and no one acted as if this was unusual. Spiritual oppression was one more evil that came upon people in a fallen world, like disease or famine. It wasn't a rarity.

It's not rare today either. But most of us aren't attuned to it. Family members and friends, as well as those in the healing professions, are quick to attribute demonic activity to causes they can make sense of: chemical imbalance or mental illness, depression, addiction, a tragic past, emotional instability, or even "eccentricity." As such, the victims are offered pills and therapy and support groups— all of which can be helpful remedies when evil spirits are not involved, but which won't remedy the problem if spiritual oppression is at the root.

Don't get me wrong: I don't see the devil under every exam table. Plenty of the things that ail people are not demonic; they are the result of living in a tainted and troubled world. Our world got this way because of Satan and his sinful influence on Adam and Eve, so we have him to blame for any evil or darkness that ever befalls us in this life. Nevertheless, that doesn't make every illness or hardship demon-driven.

I will admit one thing, though. Now that I know what I know, I see that the dark side can make an even more powerful case for the reality of heaven than the stories of healing and miracles. How? Because evil is so pervasive—we have all been exposed to it. Furthermore, when it surfaces, it is typically either in-your-face dramatic or exceedingly dark and brooding. Moderation is not its hallmark.

In its aggressive state, evil manifests as raw, ugly, rude, un-restrained, raging, or excessively harmful or inhuman words or behavior. For example, when demons are present, the oppressed person probably won't just swear occasionally; more likely, prac-tically everything that comes out of his or her mouth will be offensive, and at its worst may be as vile and nasty as anything you've ever heard. He or she won't have fleeting destructive or anxious thoughts but will probably be absolutely obsessed, and may take extreme measures to act on them. And physically speak-ing, the person under demonic influence is prone to display acute symptoms rather than just mild ones. He or she won't just be dif-ficult to calm; the patient will be almost humanly impossible to hold back. Instead of exhibiting a little confusion, the individual's actions and/or thinking will be wild and disruptive, as if his or her internal systems have gone amok.

In other words, what results when evil enters in is the exact op-posite of the pervading peace that accompanies heaven's presence.

James 3:15, 17 says that wherever you have "envy and selfish ambition, there you find disorder and every evil practice"—and these things are "earthly, unspiritual, of the devil." Conversely, "the wisdom that comes from heaven is first of all pure; then peace-loving, considerate, submissive, full of mercy and good fruit, impartial and sincere."

In its more passive form, evil may manifest as what we might call "quiet torment"—deep depression; despairing, suicidal thoughts; severe anxiety; unrelenting guilt, shame, or regret; or an over-whelming sense of rejection or abandonment.

Again, though, not every bout of depression or act of aggression is an evil spirit. We live in a natural world, not just a supernatural one. This makes us prone to the ill effects of inhabiting a planet and a physical body that is decaying under the curse of sin. We are sus-ceptible to disease, aging, unrest, uncertainty, brokenness, sadness, and pain. As you become more aware of the supernatural realm, though, you learn to discern fairly quickly between its wicked forces at work versus natural causes. If the supernatural is operating, it will make itself known in the presence of the light.

EXPOSED TO THE LIGHT

Case in point: I got a call one day from the family of a gentleman I'd treated off and on for several years. "Please come over," they pleaded. "He is dying, and we want you to pray for him. Then we're going to let him go."

When I arrived at the house, the family was assembled down-stairs, waiting for me. We collectively walked up the creaking stairs into a dim hallway, and on into the patient's bedroom. Though he was lying there very ill, seemingly in his final hours, I felt com-pelled to ask: "Mr. Martin, I know you're tired and sick. Do you want to go? Do you want to die now?"

His answer surprised me, weak though it was: "No."

"Then I'll pray that you live," I told him.

All unbelief must be removed before you pray for someone's healing. Since I didn't know the spiritual status of the family members, I excused everyone from the room. However, I was so focused on Mr. Martin that I didn't check over my shoulder to see if everyone was gone, and so I didn't realize one of his sons had stayed behind. As I prayed against the spirit of death and for the sick one's healing, I suddenly heard flapping behind me. When I turned to discover what was making the noise, I spied Mr. Martin's son writhing on the ground in full-blown demonic possession.

By the next morning, Mr. Martin had rallied and was literally up out of bed, fixing breakfast. I didn't know whether the spirit of death had left him and gone into his son, or whether it was the presence of God facing down an evil spirit that was already in the young man. In any case, the kingdom of darkness was present in that bedroom, and when the kingdom of light entered in, the darkness was exposed.

The name of Jesus and the power of the cross cause demons to reveal themselves. The way they manifest is so over-the-top and unnatural that it further strengthens my belief in the Lord every time—because for all their power, His power proves that much greater.

Heaven's might is most evident when you see people being delivered of evil spirits. This is as true now as it was in Jesus' day. Luke 9:37–43 speaks of one such incident:

When [Jesus and His disciples] came down from the mountain, a large crowd met him. A man in the crowd called out, "Teacher, I beg you to look at my son, for he is my only child. A spirit seizes him and he suddenly screams; it throws him into convulsions so that he foams at the mouth. It scarcely ever leaves him and is destroying him. I begged your disciples to drive it out, but they could not."

"You unbelieving and perverse generation," Jesus replied, "how long shall I stay with you . . . ? Bring your son here."

Even while the boy was coming, the demon threw him to the ground in a convulsion. But Jesus rebuked the impure spirit, healed the boy and gave him back to his father. And they were all amazed at the greatness of God.

Notice that last line: this revealed *the greatness of God* to those witnesses. The evil spirit showed a fierce ability to provoke upheaval and intimidation. Judging by Jesus' words, it seems that even some of His own disciples may have been frightened by the intensity of this particular spirit. But as soon as the One in whom all spiritual authority abides rebuked that spirit, it was forced to leave the boy, and he immediately was made well.

I had an encounter with a similarly intense spirit one time in my office. I later learned my patient had been involved in witchcraft in her past, but on this day, I was simply conducting what I thought was a routine examination on this woman. When we were done, I put my hand on her head to pray for her—and as soon as I spoke the name of Jesus, she growled, did a backflip, and started alternately screaming and howling and hissing. I backed off and decided not to do anything more in that setting because it would create too much havoc among the office staff. Yet I knew that, as a Catholic, she would have to go to Washington, DC, for an exorcism because none of the local churches would perform one. So instead, when she came back for a follow-up visit, I was prepared. I prayed to cast out that spirit, and she was delivered.

A while back another woman I'll call Sarah came to my office with a briefcase full of medical paperwork. The victim of recurrent seizures (which she'd thoroughly documented and which she'd had her friends film), she'd found no relief except for some help from a neurological hospital. After taking her history, I knew the origin of her problems: for years growing up, she'd been raped by male relatives, and when they would molest her, she'd go into a trance and fake seizures—called pseudo-seizures—to get the men to stop. The trauma, though, had opened the door to a more sinister problem that was about to surface.

Only minutes after I left the exam room, my assistant rushed up: "Doctor, she's having a full-blown seizure right now!" I discerned instantly what was going on, and I told my PA, "Those aren't seizures; they're demons. Go in my office and get my Bible!"

I put the Bible on Sarah's belly and prayed to rebuke the spirits that I knew were there. Sarah stopped seizing immediately.

Believing the demons had left, I started jotting down some medical notes, and it happened again.

"In the name of Jesus, Satan, I cast you out of this woman!" I yelled—and Sarah's seizures ceased again, briefly. Then they resumed once more.

By this time I'd been with her for about ninety minutes, and the entire office was disrupted. There was a backlog of other patients; the meds we'd given her to stop the seizures had no effect; and she had put up such a fight, the medical staff was exhausted. Everyone around me was starting to freak out, yet I knew I'd cast out any demons; they could no longer be operating within her.

What was going on?

Then it occurred to me: *Maybe this is flesh-driven*—meaning, the effects of old habits and psychological mechanisms she had used to cope with the abuse. Because they are an individual's "choice"—natural, protective responses to trauma—they can be helped by natural (medical) means, although it is important to continue spiritual follow-up so the demons do not return worse than before (Matt. 12:43–45).

At that point, I instructed the staff to call 911, and they took the patient to the hospital ER for treatment. They then transferred Sarah to a psychiatric hospital.

Three or four months later she came back to thank me for praying, and instantly I could tell she was a new person, inside and out. As Sarah briefed me on all that had happened since her episode in our exam room, she confirmed what I could already see: she had come to know Christ while at the psychiatric hospital, and she was also cured of her seizures.

Intrigued, I asked her: "What happened that day?"

She said, "Doc, I was loaded with demons and the last one was cast out when you prayed."

Am I afraid in these situations? Not anymore. I am well aware of the power of the darkness, but I live and work under a far greater power, and so I know I never have to be afraid. The Bible is very reassuring in this regard: "God does not give us a spirit of fear, but of power, and of love and of a sound mind" (2 Tim. 1:7 NKJV). Christians are also supplied with full-body armor for spiritual warfare (Eph. 6:10–18). All the weapons of hell are powerless against me as long as I am covered under the blood of Christ, walking in the might of heaven, and wielding the sword of the Spirit, which is the Word of God.

I will talk more specifically about this later, but the key is to know your authority in the Lord and take it—aware that the darkness cannot remain where the light of heaven falls.

OUR TRUE OPPONENT

Third World believers, who live in cultures where spiritual things are not covered over by the sophistications of education or religion, understand that we are always wrestling against the powers of darkness, and that evil spirits have to leave when we bind them up through the name of Jesus. Not so much those of us in First World countries. We are too caught up in the spirit of materialism and entitlement to realize who our true opponent is or how to combat him.

When we do recognize and cast out the enemy, though, he has to exit. And the kingdom of light moves in and takes up residence.

One mother I know—a strong believer—got to see this truth in action. Ms. Helen was in my office one day, very upset and lamenting the current state of her household. "My home life is crazy," she told me, "and I don't know what to do. One of my sons is on drugs, and my other son watches TV all day with the blinds down, refusing to let any light in. He sits in darkness all day long."

I urged her, "Take authority over that, Ms. Helen. Go into each room, pull up the blinds, turn off the TVs, and say, 'In the name of Jesus and the power of His cross, I cast you out, evil spirits, and command you to leave this place!' Then open the front door and pray it again and kick those spirits out!"

That godly mother went home and did exactly what I recommended, and her entire household was delivered from its overwhelming oppression. The next time I saw her, she had seen a complete turnaround in her kids—and the light was all over her face.

We can't ever let our guard down, however. As soon as we do, the drama will start up again.

In September 2004, when Chad came down with a tumor on his ear after a period of remission, Deborah and I both grieved. We'd been thrilled with his improved health and had stopped going to healing services and missionary conferences because life had gotten so busy while we remodeled our house. One night as Deborah prayed over Chad, she fell asleep and dreamed she saw him entering a jail cell in a trance. She screamed at him not to go in there, because she could see the devil waiting to close the door behind him. That was a wakeup call for us.

A few months later, Chad was resting without his oxygen mask when he spontaneously muttered, "A male witch is a warlock." Neither of our boys ever watched or read anything where they would've learned this, so we thought maybe it was because it was Halloween season.

Deborah nudged him and said, "Chad, wake up. Why did you say that?" With a faint laugh and a little surprised at himself, he told her, "I had a dream, and I could see you instructing Christian about a male witch."

Of course, neither Deborah nor I were involved in any such thing, and Christian was off at boarding school. However, when we phoned Christian later that day, we learned the school was hosting a guest speaker who had taught that day on mind-reading and would be teaching on levitation at a "Bible study" that evening. It was just another reminder that we must never let up or give in, because Satan and his soldiers are actively engaged against the army of God for human souls.

I tell you these things not to scare you, but because we are all in a war zone every day, and the sooner we realize it, the stronger we will be.

I fight for the physical lives of my patients—an aspect of the battle I've always understood. But now that I'm convinced of a greater realm where battles for people's eternities are constantly fought, I'm not content to strive for just their physical well-being. I join in combat every day with the army of heaven and with fellow Christians like you to call in the kingdom of light where only the kingdom of darkness has reigned.

Just as I long for my patients to escape the physical agonies of disease, I long for them to escape the eternal agonies of hell. That's why I give them the best of medicine and the best of Jesus: because that's the path to life and health, both here and beyond.

If you're a born-again believer, you have Jesus to offer your tribe too. Whoever you're fighting for—whether it's your students, your household, your community, or the impoverished or orphaned of the world—get in the Word, learn your authority... and then go forth and conquer. We Christians have all power to overtake and dispel the darkness through the Light of heaven, the Light of the world, Jesus Christ.

※

Our struggle is not against flesh and blood, but against the rulers, against the authorities, against the powers of this dark world and against the spiritual forces of evil in the heavenly realms.

Ephesians 6:12

Amazement came upon them all, and they began talking with one another saying, "What is this message? For with authority and power He commands the unclean spirits and they come out."

Luke 4:36 NASB

These are the words of the Son of God... To the one who is victorious and does my will to the end, I will give authority over the nations...just as I have received authority from my Father.

Revelation 2:18, 26–27

CHAPTER 8
RESURRECTION POWER

I REALIZE THAT the things I'm sharing are not a natural way of thinking, believing, or behaving. That's why we need a supernatural movement of God—the empowerment of the Holy Spirit, the fire of heaven—to initiate us into the workings of the realm beyond what we see.

What I've discovered is that the Lord can make available to us everything here on earth that is available in the kingdom of heaven. There is always an alternative to the darkness. And sometimes heaven's alternative is vastly beyond what we would ever imagine. That's why we mustn't shrink back from asking for the impossible...because *anything* is possible when the outcome is in heaven's hands.

Maybe you're still not sure about whether healings and miracles happen today, simply because you haven't seen these things for yourself. Admittedly, not everyone comes face-to-face with eternal realities every day like I do. Still, had I not opened myself to the possibility of divine involvement in the earthly realm, I would encounter far less of heaven than I do, and I know the impact on my patients would be greatly diminished. I'm also not sure how I would've survived what happened to my son Chad.

In light of everything heaven has permitted me to be part of, am I crazy to believe? Some people may think so, but I like what professor and philosopher Merold Westphal has said: "If God exists, miracles are not merely logically possible, but really and genuinely possible at every moment."[1]

I'm an avid student of the Bible, not a Bible scholar, so I prefer to leave the comprehensive "case for miracles" to the experts. But let me suggest at least this: if you can believe even a few things about God, you can believe He does miracles. Josh McDowell put it this way: "The basis for believing in the miraculous goes back to the biblical concept of God. The very first verse of the Bible decides the issue: 'In the beginning God created the heavens and the earth' (Genesis 1:1 RSV). If this verse can be accepted at face value... then the rest should not be a problem."[2]

In other words, if you can conceive that God has the power to create universes and galaxies and planets and entire populations of people, then it really isn't much of a leap to allow that He has the power to heal the human body. And if He can heal our bodies—restoring what was damaged, making broken parts whole again—then why shouldn't we think He is capable of the greatest of miracles: resurrecting men, women, and children from the dead? On the other hand, if you won't accept the message of the gospel, as simple as it is, you won't believe greater things about God even if you were to see someone's life restored.

Nevertheless, from the prophets of old to Jesus and His disciples, the servants of the Lord have been bringing the dead back to life for centuries. Scripture records numerous accounts of this without equivocation. What sets the resurrection of Jesus apart from all the others who have been brought back from the dead, however, is that, once raised, He never died again. Romans 6:9 says: "Since Christ was raised from the dead, he cannot die again; death no longer has mastery over him." Truly, He conquered death.

Because of Him, every believer will one day step from this life into eternal life with Him in Paradise. Because of Him, every believer has access to the resurrection power of heaven.

POWER FOR TODAY

Having learned how reliable the Bible is, I was able to accept the veracity of its raised-from-the-dead stories. But I hadn't really considered whether that miracle still happened today—until I witnessed a few of these miracles myself. By then, even if I'd been inclined to deny it, I just couldn't. Neither could the medical professionals around me.

Nowadays, if you ask me whether the power of heaven extends to restoring the dead to life, I can answer without hesitation—because I have seen it happen. More than once.

Our son Christian arrived from boarding school late one afternoon in October 2004 and came right over to see Chad in the hospital in Houston. Chad's skin was bruised and raw from radiation treatments, his coloring was pale, and he had lost considerable weight. Shocked at how much his brother had declined, Christian rubbed Chad's head, made him laugh a little, and began to feed him a smoothie with a straw.

Once the boys had visited, Deborah took Christian to the apartment to get unpacked. A few hours later, Chad had a strange reaction to some of his medicine. When Deborah returned to his bedside, his eyes looked distant and something about him seemed off.

That night was one of spiritual warfare. Chad did not rest at all, and neither did his mother.

As soon as I got to his bedside, I stood over Chad and rebuked the devil—and Chad finally fell asleep. Yet come the morning, he was weaker than he'd ever been, and his blood pressure continued to weaken.

Deborah leaned over to him, hoping he could hear, and said loudly, "Chad, I love you...I love you...I love you!"

He smiled with half-opened eyes and responded, "I love you too." And then he closed his eyes again—but he was different. Not okay. His body went limp in a way and his eyes seemed slightly fixed in a way we'd never seen.

"He doesn't look right. Is he asleep?" Deborah asked apprehensively. I too registered that something was seriously wrong, so I stepped out to get help.

In just a matter of moments, the word from the medical team was heart-wrenching: "He's gone."

Instantly, Deborah knelt beside Chad's bed, pulling him over her shoulder. Jesus' words to His entombed friend came immediately to her mind—"Lazarus, come forth" (John 11:43 kjv)—and she began praying in Chad's ear, taking authority over the enemy and demanding, "In the name of Jesus, Chad, I call you back! Come forth, Chad, in Jesus' name!"

The Holy Spirit spontaneously reminded her of additional Scripture, and she overflowed with a fountain of life-giving words from the Word of God that she had stored up in her heart: "You shall not die but live, and declare the works of the Lord! With long life, Chad, God will satisfy you and show you His salvation!..." (Ps. 118:17; 91:16, her paraphrase).

I had never seen a mother fight for her child in the heavenly realm the way Deborah was doing. Her devotion to Chad and her trust in the promises of the Lord merged in those moments of unceasing prayer—and while it was an agonizing and fearful situation, it was also a beautiful picture that has never left my mind. It was as if, while she held our son, heaven and its glory were holding her.

I was astounded at the breadth of Deborah's scriptural recall. She prayed a torrent of verses in just a few minutes' time. And in this instance, heaven said yes: as quickly as Chad had gone, he returned. The first thing his mother noticed was that his ears regained their color.

Both the lead nurse and the respiratory tech remarked at how unprecedented this was in their experience. "You prayed over your boy, and he's alive!" the tech announced.

Deborah laid Chad back on his pillow and looked at his side: what had just minutes before been black and blue and purple and raw was now pink and nearly all healed! And when the nurses re-took Chad's vitals, his levels were back to normal.

I wanted to be sure, so I grabbed his hand and said, "Chad, if you can hear me, squeeze my hand." My son's response was instant. He was back.

The lessons in this were hard for me to miss. First, the Word of the Lord has great authority and power—the power of life over death and victory over defeat. Second, I knew I needed to be even more fervent in my study and memorization of Scripture.

Two years later, on October 20, 2006, God reinforced these spir-itual lessons for me all over again. I called my wife from work and said, "You're not going to believe what just happened this morn-ing..." But of course, she could believe it—and she did! I was the one who needed to wrap my head around it.

A middle-aged mechanic named Jeff Markin had come to the ER at Palm Beach Gardens Medical Center, complaining of an un-settled stomach and chest pain. He also couldn't catch his breath. While he was filling out admissions paperwork, his breathing quickened and became more shallow—and then suddenly he passed out and fell hard to the floor, dead.

The ER team surrounded him and began life-saving measures. I was in the surgical wing of the hospital, prepping several patients for heart procedures, when a "code blue" was announced over the intercom. A few minutes later, a voice came back on: "Dr. Cran-dall, report to the ER immediately. Dr. Crandall to the ER."

What I walked into was a disaster area. Total chaos. A war zone.

Every available member of our staff was crammed into that small emergency exam room, trying to counter the effects of a major heart attack. They'd been working on the patient for thirty minutes already—inserting IV lines, intubating Jeff so he could breathe, in-jecting his heart with meds, shocking him with the defibrillator—all in a valiant effort to keep his heart beating and his brain supplied with oxygen.

Six, seven...ten times they shocked him. Still he wouldn't

breathe and we couldn't get his heartbeat back. He was also cyanotic: his extremities—toes, fingers, nails, lips—were turning black, dying.

After nearly three-quarters of an hour with no change and no response, the physician on duty looked to me—the heart specialist and senior cardiologist on duty that day—to make the call. This is the proper procedure in a cardiac case.

"Let's call the code," I said in surrender. "There's nothing more to do."

Jeff Markin's time of death was recorded as 8:05 a.m.

I stayed in the room a while longer to complete the paperwork while one of the nurses began to disconnect all the wires and clean up the body for the morgue. When I was finished, I headed toward the door to return to the surgical wing. But just as I got to the doorway, I was caught short by a command; I felt the Lord telling me, "Turn around and pray for that man." I paused and then started again on my way, and the same message came a second time to me: "Turn around and pray for that man."

I questioned, *Lord, what do I pray for? He's dead!*

Even though the rational part of me was shouting how absurd this was, I knew I was hearing the quiet but forceful voice of heaven, and I needed to respond. Still, I went through a gamut of mental gymnastics in just a few seconds: *What's the point of this? It's crazy! Can I somehow do it without the nurse seeing, and without looking like a fool? How do I even find the words?*

Somehow, God helped me set all those concerns aside and pray anyway. I was discreet about it, but I did it. I walked back over to the stretcher, leaned over that dead body, and said, "Father God, if this man doesn't know You as his Lord and Savior, I ask that you raise him from the dead now, in Jesus' name." The next thing I knew, my right arm was spontaneously lifted toward heaven as if it was on an invisible pulley—and while I was still in that posture of worship, the ER doctor reentered the room.

"Shock him one more time," I told my colleague.

"But Dr. Crandall, he's dead! We've already shocked him a dozen times."

"Do it for me," I pleaded. "Please. Just once more."

He warily obliged, probably just to get me to let this go. Yet when those defibrillator paddles sent their electrical currents into Jeff's chest, suddenly the solid line on the electrocardiogram spiked. We had a heartbeat! And it was followed by another and another, in a regular rhythm that never misfired (which in itself is almost unheard of after what Jeff's heart had been through).

As I watched heaven's power resurrect this man, his abdomen twitched first and then his chest filled with air. Then his fingers and toes moved, and soon he let out a gush of air from his mouth.

The attending nurse wailed—and not just for a moment. *She let loose!* And she stared at me, eyes bulging, like I was an alien. When she stopped screaming, she was absolutely beside herself. "Doctor, what have you done? What are we supposed to do?"

I replied with the only thing I could think of: "I don't know— let's get him to ICU! Stat!"

Jeff's recovery was truly miraculous. When I visited him on Monday, you wouldn't have known that a mere seventy-two hours earlier, he'd been another fatality. The only telltale signs were his darkened fingers and toes.

It is nearly a decade later, and Jeff is still with us. Best of all, not long after God intersected our lives in that ER exam room, He fulfilled His purpose for bringing this man back to life: Jeff accepted Christ as his Lord and Savior.

Heaven's resurrection power extends to our soul and spirit, not just our body. That kind of truth should motivate us all to greater boldness in the face of the enemy.

IF YOU WILL PRAY...

The case that probably most radically advanced my belief in *all* of heaven's power and possibilities, however, happened in 2012.

Mike Williams was a husband and father in his early fifties. After completing a video workout one morning, he transitioned to his treadmill and, after a few minutes, he collapsed. When his wife and children heard him fall, they came running. His boys had taken CPR training as part of their lifeguard certification, so they did chest compressions and breathed for their dad until an ambulance arrived. The emergency technicians recognized that Mike was in cardiac arrest, so they shocked him multiple times, but he had suffered anoxic brain injury—massive damage that occurs when the brain is deprived of sufficient oxygen for four to five minutes or more—and he was declared brain-dead at the hospital.

His family was devastated, but they also had exceeding faith, and so, despite his prognosis, they prayed. They asked others to join them in prayer too.

The day after Mike was admitted to our hospital, somebody asked me to stop by and pray for him. Though Mike wasn't on my cardiac service, I am always willing to pray for other doctors' patients.

When I walked into his room, it was apparent to me that, clinically speaking, he'd been down too long. Not only were his face and hands contorted and swollen, but he was on ventilation and every form of life support, showing absolutely no signs of awareness and no movement. I read his chart and reviewed his records, and the facts were overwhelming: this patient was far, far gone. Still, I dutifully prayed, even though I had little faith because his brain injury was so severe.

The next day Kristi, a friend of Deborah's, called and asked if I would pray for a friend of their family's named Mike Williams. "The neurologist wants to take him off the ventilator because he's showing no signs of life apart from the machines," she reported. Deb passed along the message to me, and I told her, "I know who you're talking about; I've prayed for him already. That man is brain-dead, and I really don't think he's got a chance. There's just nothing more to be done for him."

Deborah asked me to go back and pray for him again the next

day, and the next, and so on. I was thinking, *No, the guy's gone*, but I didn't want to upset my wife, so I did as she asked. Some of the nurses were mad at me, fearful that if he did somehow, miraculously, respond and start to breathe on his own, he would be only a shell, which might be even more traumatizing to his family. Three of Mike's doctors agreed he was not going to revive, but they needed his wife's consent to remove life support, and she wouldn't give it. She kept insisting that he would live if people would pray.

Every day for two weeks, I went and prayed for Mike, and as expected, nothing changed—he didn't move a muscle or come out of his coma. Then one day Mike's wife called me, elated: "Doctor Crandall, he's moving! Mike moved!"

Hoping this wasn't a loved one's wishful thinking, I talked to the charge nurse, and she confirmed: "Yes, Mr. Williams is responsive." Still, the medical staff was rightfully cautious. A little movement did not guarantee wellness or even the remotest quality of life, and no one wanted to get the family's hopes up. A few of the nurses told me privately, "His wife is crazy, thinking he's going to ever walk again."

Yet the good reports continued to pour in.

In time, Mike got off the ventilator entirely, and now he is back home with his wife and kids—a living, breathing, talking, walking, resurrected miracle.

After Mike, I told Deborah, "From this point on, I will step into faith and rely on the Word of God and proclaim *it* rather than what is before my eyes. His Word is greater than any facts I can ever be presented with."

Mike's story was very faith-building for me, bringing my spiritual understanding to another level and sparking a greater pursuit of God. It was as if the Lord said, "Your discovery phase is over. You've seen it all, experienced it all, heard it all. Now come back to my Word." So now I study the Scriptures constantly. They are written on my heart. I know the truth, and I walk in it. Daily.

That truth says the Lord will deliver His people from the power of the grave and redeem them from death. It says that Christians serve the One who conquered death, and that in Him we have all power. It says Jesus declared Himself to be the resurrection and the life, and because of Him, we have hope.

From here on out, I will ever believe my God is Healer and Deliverer. I will not give up on Him no matter what things look like. I will hold on to Him and keep pursuing Him till the absolute end.

FAITH, NOT SIGHT

All three of these death-to-life encounters really brought home to me how much of the Christian journey is one of faith rather than sight. The power of heaven is believing for the possibilities beyond what we can see or know in the natural world. It centers on understanding that when the Word of God says we have all the forces of heaven behind us—even the power to call forth life—we can count on it to be true.

Regardless of a doctor's prognosis or the silence of a pulse or the numbers from a lab test, we must pray in full belief that heaven's authority will come down. Even if we're presented with the impossible, God's Word still takes authority over that. Now I can go into any situation where death seems to have the upper hand, assured that "I've seen this before, I know Who wins, and I can proclaim the Word over it."

That doesn't mean every flatlined heart will renew its pulse, or that every promise of God unconditionally applies at face value to every situation. No, He is still sovereign, and He decides when to restore life—either now or future, in this life or in eternity. Still, in our going forth and declaring what God has said in Scripture, the resurrection life of Jesus cannot be stopped. It breaks through earth's darkness, conquering death and suffering with heaven's light and peace, healing and comfort.

Genesis 1 says that at the time of Creation, the Holy Spirit hovered over the waters, and when the word was spoken, life burst forth. The Holy Spirit presently waits for us to speak the Word into the void left by the enemy. When we do, the Word never returns empty. It yields life somehow, some way.

Here's one other important thing that Mike's case taught me—and hopefully this will encourage you too. It was one of those times when I didn't hear the voice of God within my own spirit. Clearly, the Lord was compelling others to pray without ceasing, and urging me through them to do the same, but I didn't get the message directly. Thankfully, I no longer have to hear the voice of God to know He will bring His Word to fruition. I know because the Bible tells me so. I just need to pray—believing, trusting, resting. He will be faithful to finish His work and fulfill His Word.

❧

With great power the apostles continued to testify to the resurrection of the Lord Jesus.

Acts 4:33

If the Spirit of him who raised Jesus from the dead is living in you, he who raised Christ from the dead will also give life to your mortal bodies because of his Spirit who lives in you.

Romans 8:11

Jesus looked at them and said, "With man this is impossible, but with God all things are possible."

Matthew 19:26

So will My word be which goes forth from My mouth; it will not return to Me empty, without accomplishing what I desire, and without succeeding in the matter for which I sent it.

Isaiah 55:11 NASB

PART II

THE TRUTH ABOUT HEAVEN AND THE AFTERLIFE

CHAPTER 9

THE *REAL* REAL WORLD

I'VE KNOWN PLENTY of churchgoing people who have grown up on the Bible and its stories. They know it so well, they can rattle off verse after verse that they've tucked away in their memory. But the words didn't become real to them until their experiences backed up what they'd been reading their entire lives.

For them, they know the truth—and then they believe. I did the reverse: my life experiences had to prove the truth first. Then I really started to examine the Bible and found that it confirmed what I was wondering about and witnessing. Especially in regard to heaven. As I searched the Scriptures and read pastors and scholars who have spent their lives researching heaven, my understanding of it crystallized.

Deb too has said, "God blessed me by assigning me the task of teaching the Bible. When I would find verses that reflected our experience with Chad or in ministry, it helped me understand how great the connection between heaven and earth is."

Even with all the glimmers I've had of heaven, I am decidedly aware that they are only a pale reflection, a clouded mirror (1 Cor. 13:12) of all that is and is to come for those who accept Christ's offer of eternal life. My patients and I have been touched by the slightest rays of heaven's glory, witnessed what amounts to the first tiny stroke of the first letter of its full alphabet of truth. Yet these microscopic peeks have made me long for it beyond anything I've ever desired. Because one day I will be face-to-face with my Savior and Creator, united with Him and reunited with my son and other loved ones who made it home before me.

The testimonies of those today who claim to have touched heaven must be tested against Scripture, but we can utterly rely on the testimony of Scripture itself. When I couple their snapshots with the words of Jesus, who alone had experienced the infinite, inexpressible glories of heaven in all their fullness, I gain a far greater picture of what to expect. The experiences of so many biblical figures who encountered heaven in some way only add to my confidence. And the wisdom of faithful men and women of the Word through the centuries have further helped clarify what I've read.

In these next three chapters, let me consolidate some of what I've learned as I've studied the truth about what's to come, its impact on our thinking, and what it means for how we live.

"FOREVER" IS IMPRINTED IN THE HUMAN HEART.

Like any loving father, God wants His family complete and gathered together with Him, and so He has instilled eternity in our hearts (Eccl. 3:11). Not in the physical, human heart, but in the soul.

The human body is "only a container," according to Bishop Keith Butler—a priceless, complex, magnificently created container, for sure, yet one with an expiration date. Meanwhile, the infinite part of us longs to return to the Eden we lost, where we can once again be in the presence of God, perfectly loved and perfectly safe, forever. This thirst runs so deep that author Mark Buchanan has called it "the ache in our bones." Many writers have referred to it as "homesickness" of the most fundamental kind.

Not everyone can articulate this yearning to be settled in a far better place, face-to-face with the Creator, but people of all eras and cultures and religions have written about it, sung of it, painted it, imagined it. Home is their true longing! And as C. S. Lewis explained, "If I find in myself a desire which no experience in this world can satisfy, the most probable explanation is that I was made for another world."[1]

Why does this reality matter? Mother Teresa once remarked: "People ask me about death and whether I look forward to it and I answer, 'Of course,' because I am going home."[2]

Heaven displaces our mortal dread with boldness and security as we walk this earth. We know this life is short and our world is fraught with danger. If not for the life we have in God, "our days on earth are like a shadow, without hope" (1 Chron. 29:15). One of Job's friends rightfully said of anyone who forgets God: "While still growing and uncut, they wither more quickly than grass... What they trust in is fragile; what they rely on is a spider's web. They lean on the web, but it gives way; they cling to it, but it does not hold" (Job 8:12–15). But John could testify to his fellow Christians: "I write these things to you who believe in the name of the Son of God that you may know that you have eternal life" (1 John 5:13).

Having assurance of eternal life puts it all in perspective. Whatever difficulty surrounds me now, this too shall pass. Whatever opposition I face today, it will one day soon be defeated. "For the form of this world is passing away" (1 Cor. 7:31 NKJV); "the darkness is passing away and the true light is already shining" (1 John 2:8). And someday future, "God will wipe away every tear... there shall be no more death, nor sorrow, nor crying. There shall be no more pain" (Rev. 21:4 NKJV), and we will be face-to-face with Him (1 John 3:2).

To live *in* Christ means that I can continue to be "fruitful" for the length of my days on this earth (Phil. 1:22 NLT); to live *for* Christ means that "to die is gain"—my demise is a promotion, a beginning, not a demotion or loss (Phil. 1:21). The surety of heaven has fortified Christ's disciples in every era to complete their life's work and endure every form of persecution and threat. It also enabled

Jesus to take up His cross in full faith (Matt. 26:39, 42; Heb. 12:2). Cancer survivor and bestselling author Sarah Young has journaled: "When I'm dealing with multiple trials, this cord is a lifeline protecting me from despair. As I cling to hope in the midst of trouble, I am able to perceive You [Jesus] cheering me on: encouraging me with the absolute certainty of heaven."[3]

EVERY HUMAN IS GUARANTEED A FOREVER; IT'S JUST A MATTER OF WHERE "FOREVER" WILL BE SPENT.

Scripture says, "People are destined to die once, and after that to face judgment" (Heb. 9:27–28). The ungodly, the rebellious "will go away into eternal punishment, but the righteous into eternal life" (Matt. 25:46 NASB).

Our God is "from everlasting to everlasting" (Ps. 90:2 NKJV), and He has given immortality to the sons and daughters of earth, the beloved of His creation. "There are no ordinary people," C. S. Lewis reminded us; everyone we see, meet, or know is an immortal being, destined to live out eternity in Satan's realm or God's.[4]

Here, then, is the reality: from the time we are conceived, we are on course to eternity. Yes, we have a layover on earth, but as soon as we touch down in this world, the clock commences ticking off the hours in anticipation of our final departure. If we are afforded the average lifespan, we will have just under 615,000 hours until takeoff—a matter of some 25,000 days. How quickly it goes! And as quickly as we make our entrance, we are on our way out, headed to our final destination.

I've heard Reinhard Bonnke say, "The border to eternity runs parallel to this life and is just one step away. It may be crossed over any time by anybody." The question is: What are we going to do with that? We have to make a choice.

Depending on which side of eternity's question you take, death is either dreadful or desirable; the greatest loss or the consummate gain. Charles Spurgeon preached, "Death to the wicked is the King of terrors. Death to the saint is the end of terrors, the com-

mencement of glory."[5] No one can anticipate advantage, bene-
fit, profit in death—except for the Christian. If we don't live for
Christ, dying means hell.

Eternal *life* begins the moment a person accepts Christ's gift of
salvation; earth's death then becomes a graduation day into every
aspect of that blessing. Those who do nothing except to keep walking in the sin of the flesh will one day find themselves resurrected
to judgment, banned forever to the lake of fire (John 5:28–29 NASB;
Rev. 20:15).

Thankfully, the entrance to everlasting life is just as close as eternity itself, reminds Reinhard Bonnke: "Jesus is the door and 'today
is the day of salvation'" (see Luke 13:24; 2 Cor. 6:2 NKJV). How
do we attain eternal life? Repentance, faith, and trust in Christ for
salvation (Matt. 3:2; John 3:16; Acts 13:38–39).

The stakes are high surrounding this decision about where to
spend forever. "One minute after you slip behind the parted curtain," offers Pastor Erwin Lutzer, "you will either be enjoying a
personal welcome from Christ or catching your first glimpse of
doom as you have never known it."[6]

You're either here on earth, or you're there in the eternal realm.
There's no middle ground. Within an instant—in one heartbeat—
you can be on the other side of eternity. And whether you step
into eternal life or eternal death depends on what you decide about
Christ: If you choose Him as your Lord and Deliverer, you will
spend forever with Him in heaven. If you refuse Him, you will forever languish in hell and be separated from Him.

ETERNAL LIFE IS A FACT, AND THIS IS EVERY CHRISTIAN'S DESTINY.[7]

For eternal life to be true, death has to have been defeated. Almost
no event in ancient history has been as thoroughly documented, or
as thoroughly investigated, as Christ's death and resurrection. His
actual death, burial, empty tomb, and post-resurrection appearances
have been scrutinized by the faithful and foes alike—from scientists

and engineers to historians and theologians and skeptics. And "no miracle has as much historical evidence to confirm it," cite Norman Geisler and Ron Brooks.[8]

When I as a surgeon read the gospel records about the bodily fluids Jesus lost, the nature of His wounds, and the injuries He sustained both before and during His crucifixion—including the soldier's spear that clearly perforated both his lung and his heart—I can tell you: Jesus did indeed die. Historians confirm that His executioners, who were experts in death by crucifixion, didn't break His legs as they usually did for one simple reason: because they could see that He was already dead as He hung on the cross (John 19:32–33).

His corpse was then customarily wrapped in up to a hundred pounds of linen and embalming spices sealed with myrrh and placed in a sealed stone tomb with only one access point. The weight of the rock over the entrance has been estimated at nearly two thousand pounds; it had to be rolled into place with the help of gravity, it was so heavy.

Christ's opponents knew He had foretold of His resurrection (Matt. 27:63–66), so the tomb was guarded around the clock by Roman soldiers (likely sixteen or more), precisely so that Christ's disciples could not steal His body and conduct a hoax. Nevertheless, Jesus physically arose from His grave, leaving His burial place empty on that Sunday morning except for His graveclothes. The response of the Roman guards and rulers, as well as the Jewish religious leaders—His staunch enemies who would've gone to any length to expose a deception—attest to the reliability of the biblical record (Matt. 28:11–15).

Finally, He appeared, spoke, and even taught in a resurrected body in different settings to hundreds of people over the course of forty days. Of Christ's twelve appearances, seven of them involved multiple witnesses, not just one or two individuals (Matt. 28:9–10, 16–20; Luke 24:33–49; John 20:26–30; John 21; Acts 1:49; 1 Cor. 15:6–8). Many of these people were still alive and able to confirm what they'd seen when the gospel accounts were circulated decades later. And as Josh McDowell has suggested in *A Ready Defense*, their reactions not only authentically varied from fear to wonderment to worship, but some of them, like Thomas and Jesus' brother James, were skeptical or—as in the case of Saul of Tarsus—outright "hostile," until face-to-face with the risen Jesus.[9]

So Jesus actually died and rose again; He didn't just nearly die and fake a resurrection. And He came from eternity's glorious dwelling in the first place: "I have come down from heaven, not to do My own will, but the will of Him who sent Me" (John 6:38 NKJV). Therefore, His words about heaven and life eternal are trustworthy.

We also have accounts of others that reinforce the fact of eternal life. In an early reference to heaven, Genesis 5:24 says God took Enoch. Hebrews 11:5 helps us understand what this means: "By faith Enoch was taken away so that he did not experience death." God removed Enoch from a world of sin and sorrow to a place—a permanent existence—where death could not touch him. Second Kings 2:11 speaks of Elijah, who was taken up by a whirlwind to heaven. And in Luke 9:28–36, Moses—who died a natural death (Deut. 34:5, 7–8)—and Elijah were briefly dispatched from heaven ("in glorious splendor"; Luke 9:30) to meet with Jesus on the Mount of Transfiguration. Could the three apostles who accompanied Him that day doubt the reality of eternal life? They saw and heard the two foremost prophets of the faith, long departed from this earth, conversing with Jesus about His pending death.

HEAVEN IS REAL, AND THIS IS EVERY BELIEVER'S GLORIOUS DESTINATION.

The Bible's first reference to heaven is in its very first verse: "In the beginning, God created the heavens and the earth" (Gen. 1:1). The mention of "heavens" isn't just speaking of the sky that we eye from earth, writes Pastor John Hagee. In the Hebrew, the word is a feminine plural, meaning more than one heaven.

According to Hagee in his new book, Scripture refers to three heavens. The first is the celestial "roof" above our heads here on this planet—the atmosphere, the firmament, outer space; home to the sun, moon, stars, galaxies, and constellations (e.g., Job 35:11; Ps. 8:3–4; Ps. 147:8; Dan. 7:2). The second is the supernatural realm in which the spiritual forces of heaven and hell wage war (Rev. 12:7). The third and highest one—the one the apostles Paul and John saw in their separate visions—is what we traditionally call heaven. The third heaven, which the Bible sometimes refers to as "the heights of heaven" or "the heaven of heavens" (see Job 22:12; 2 Chron. 2:6 NKJV), houses the everlasting city from which God reigns over all of heaven and earth, assisted by his angelic host.[10] This city is lit up by the Lamb of God (Rev. 21:23), with entrances of solid pearl and throughways of gold and the throne room of God (Rev. 21:21; 4:2–6, 8). Because it is the place where Jesus ascended after His resurrection and lives today (Mark 16:19), it is the eternal dwelling place of every son and daughter of God (John 6:53–58).

How can Christians be sure this is their destination? For one, because Jesus said so—and empirically proved it. Jesus said, "There is more than enough room in my Father's home. If this were not so, would I have told you that I am going to prepare a place for you?" (John 14:2 NLT).

He conquered physical death and then ascended to heaven while witnesses watched, with angels verifying: "Men of Galilee, why do you stand looking into heaven? This Jesus, who was taken up from you into heaven, will come in the same way" (Acts 1:9–11 ESV; see also John 16:28; 1 Thess. 4:14–16).

Some of the biblical writers recorded visions of heaven that were sent by heaven: the prophet Isaiah in Isaiah 6; the apostle Paul in 2 Corinthians 12; and John the apostle in Revelation. The leading figures of Scripture also laid claim to a heaven—and found comfort in its existence. Among them:

- Abraham acted in faith because He knew heaven awaited (Gen. 13; Heb. 11:9–10).
- Bildad declared: "Dominion and awe belong to God; he establishes order in the heights of heaven" (Job 25:2).
- The psalmist wrote that while Israel wandered the wilderness after the exodus from Egypt, God "rained down...the grain of heaven"—manna—for them to eat (Ps. 78:24).
- David said: "The LORD has established his throne in heaven, and his kingdom rules over all" (Ps. 103:19).
- Isaiah reported: "I saw the LORD, high and exalted, seated on a throne; and the train of his robe filled the temple. Above him were seraphim, each with six wings...And they were calling to one another: 'Holy, holy, holy is the LORD Almighty; the whole earth is full of his glory.' At the sound of their voices the doorposts and thresholds shook and the temple was filled with smoke" (Isa. 6:1–4).
- The angels who appeared to the shepherds proclaimed: "Glory to God in the highest heaven" (Luke 2:14).
- Christianity's first martyr, Stephen, "saw the glory of God" as he was being stoned and with his last breaths uttered, "Look...I see heaven open and the Son of Man standing at the right hand of God" (Acts 7:54–56).
- To "be away from the body" is to "be at home with the Lord," explained Paul to the believers in Corinth (2 Cor. 5:8 ESV).
- Paul wrote in Philippians 3:20, "Our citizenship is in heaven, from which we also eagerly wait for a Savior, the Lord Jesus Christ" (NASB).
- The apostle exhorted the family of God: "Set your sights on the realities of heaven, where Christ sits in the place of honor at God's right hand" (Col. 3:1 NLT).
- Hebrews 11 says of the members of Christianity's Hall of Fame—which include Abel, Noah, Sarah, Isaac, Jacob, Moses, and Rahab: "All these people died still believing what God had promised them. They did not receive what was promised, but

they saw it all from a distance and welcomed it. They agreed that they were foreigners and nomads here on earth. Obviously people who say such things are looking forward to a country they can call their own. If they had longed for the country they came from, they could have gone back. But they were looking for a better place, a heavenly homeland. That is why God is not ashamed to be called their God, for he has prepared a city for them" (vv. 13–16 NLT).

- Peter declared: "All praise to God, the Father of our Lord Jesus Christ. It is by his great mercy that we have been born again, because God raised Jesus Christ from the dead. Now we live with great expectation, and we have a priceless inheritance—an inheritance that is kept in heaven for you, pure and unde-filed, beyond the reach of change and decay. And through your faith, God is protecting you by his power until you receive this salvation, which is ready to be revealed on the last day for all to see" (1 Pet. 1:3–5 NLT).

- John's vision included this: "I saw a new heaven and a new earth, for the old heaven and the old earth had disap-peared...And I saw the holy city, the new Jerusalem, coming down from God out of heaven like a bride beautifully dressed for her husband. I heard a loud shout from the throne, saying, "Look, God's home is now among his people! He will live with them, and they will be his people. God himself will be with them...And the one sitting on the throne said, "Look, I am making everything new!"...And he also said, "It is fin-ished! I am the Alpha and the Omega—the Beginning and the End. To all who are thirsty I will give freely from the springs of the water of life. All who are victorious will inherit all these blessings, and I will be their God, and they will be my chil-dren" (Rev. 21:1–3, 5–7 NLT).

Heaven was known by the patriarchs and the prophets, the poets and the apostles—and Jesus brought it to light in His resurrection and ascension. According to Scripture, the certainty of the place is clear. If our preparation is equally clear, we have nothing to fear in life or in death.

BECAUSE ETERNAL LIFE IN HEAVEN AWAITS, GOD'S PEOPLE MUST KEEP ETERNITY IN MIND TODAY.

Most of us are familiar with the adage "You reap what you sow." But do you know what God's Word says specifically about sowing and reaping? "He who sows to his flesh will...reap corruption, but he who sows to the Spirit will...reap everlasting life" (Gal. 6:8 NKJV). This tells me that how I live my "now" impacts how I will spend my "then," eternally.

When we know our future in heaven lies ahead, eternity becomes our filter for all the things of earth. Being "raised to new life in Christ" raises every believer's standards. We begin to "set [our] sights on the realities of heaven," to "think about the things of heaven, not the things of earth" (Col. 3:1–2 NLT). Both our hearts and our minds are engaged in this process.

Practically stated, this means living today with lasting treasures in view. If we are heavenly minded, our thoughts cannot help but shape the way we live from day to day.

(1) *We will adjust our attitudes*, understanding that while we are "pilgrims" who are away from our true home—"aliens," "strangers" in a foreign land (1 Peter 1:1; 2:11)—we are already citizens of heaven and members of God's household (Eph. 2:18–19). Peter had a very pointed purpose for using the wording he did. He wanted us to be clear about the mindset we need while still in this world: believers are not earth-dwellers; we are heaven-bound.

Country artist Carrie Underwood's song "Temporary Home" captures this perspective.[11] Every weary traveler just wants to get home and be with loved ones. It's the place where you belong; where people know *you*—they don't just know *of* you—and you're surrounded by the things that bring you joy and comfort. You don't get that when you're just passing through a place.

We long for permanence; we have a craving to settle down and not keep wandering, ever on the move. Heaven holds out the assurance of all this and more, providing a home base from which we can operate in this life.

(2) *We will make changes to our lifestyle*—not worrying over material things or temporary achievements, but investing in what lasts: the care and salvation of people. Rather than seeking our own celebrity, we will seek justice for others. Rather than slaving over our work, we will work to deliver others from the enemy's oppression. Rather than looking out for our wants, we will "look after widows and orphans in their distress" (James 1:27). These are the values of heaven.

In his excellent book *One Minute After You Die*, Erwin Lutzer says: "Thinking about our final destination gives us perspective...Every one of us wants to make wise investments, to get the 'biggest bang for our buck.'...The best investments are those that are safe and permanent; if we are wise, we will spend our time preparing for that which lasts forever."[12]

Christian blogger Jeremy Binns has written: "I think that maybe the greater point that God is making when He speaks of streets of gold, gates of pearl, and a host of other rare and costly building materials is that those things that so many value and exchange their lives for on earth are, by comparison, merely the things to be trampled underfoot in the economy of heaven. Maybe God is really challenging us to NOT spend our lives exclusively pursing what will one day be the dust under [our] feet."[13]

The world's treasures have limited value; they fade, decay, or rust...and then they're gone. If you want to know what your earthly priorities should be, look to your Father in heaven: "A father to the fatherless, a defender of widows, is God in his holy dwelling. God sets the lonely in families, he leads out the prisoners with singing" (Ps. 68:5–6). British missionary C. T. Studd summed it this way:

Only one life, 'twill soon be past,
Only what's done for Christ will last.[14]

Holding on too tightly to earthly things will weigh us down. Holding loosely to the stuff of earth sets us free. The truth of earth is that whatever we store up here will one day be burned up. Heaven keeps our eyes on the eternal prize.

(3) *We will find help for our souls.* Second Corinthians 4:17 says: "Our light affliction, which is but for a moment, is working for us a far more exceeding and eternal weight of glory" (NKJV). "Note the contrasts Paul presented," advises Bible commentator Warren Wiersbe: "Light affliction—weight of glory; momentary—eternal; working against us—working for us. Paul...was weighing the present trials against the future glory, and he discovered that his trials were actually working for him."[15]

Our hearts will not endure the difficulties of this life without heaven before us. But because God eases the weight of our troubles and produces life from our pain and disappointment, we don't lose heart. We don't give in. We don't walk away from Him. And we don't live as those without hope (e.g., Prov. 23:18; Isa. 40:31; Jer. 29:11; Rom. 5:2; 8:28; Eph. 2:12–13; 1 Thess 4:13–14).

A heavenly perspective helps in our current situation, whatever it is: "We know that God, who raised the Lord Jesus, will also raise us with Jesus and present us to himself together with you...And as God's grace reaches more and more people, there will be great thanksgiving, and God will receive more and more glory. That is why we never give up. Though our bodies are dying, our spirits are being renewed every day" (2 Cor. 4:14–16 NLT).

4) *We will work wholeheartedly, and wait with expectancy.* Author Ted Dekker has noted this about the apostle Paul: "Having been given a glimpse of the bliss that awaits us (2 Corinthians 12:4), Paul lived a life obsessed with that day when he would have his full inheritance. Any such encounter...will surely bend any man to a fanaticism for...the hope of glory."[16]

To have eternity in view means to live and work as Paul did, and as the faithful servant did in Matthew 24:44–51. Expectant living is righteous living—doing one's wholehearted best to do the whole will of God. Expectant living also means "we fix our gaze on things that cannot be seen," knowing that "the things we cannot see will last forever" (2 Cor. 4:18 NLT).

As sons and daughters, our heavenly Father exhorts us to work passionately alongside Him in the field of souls—and to keep working until He comes or until He calls us home. "Be faithful, even to the point of death, and I will give you life as your victor's crown," He promised (Rev. 2:10; see also 3:11).

That doesn't often happen with our work on earth. We don't always get the raise we're due or receive credit for our work. But in heaven, our every kingdom-expanding act here on earth will be remembered and rewarded (Rev. 22:12). Says Pastor Steve Berger: "Some Christians will get rewards and responsibilities in heaven that will blow their minds. Why? Because [on earth] their hearts were motivated by heaven."[17]

The work won't always be easy, but the joy will never dim. And the rewards? Well, they're out of this world!

"What we suffer now is nothing compared to the glory he will reveal to us later . . . All creation is waiting eagerly for that future day when God will reveal who his children really are" (Rom. 8:18–19 NLT). "Blessed is the one who perseveres under trial because, having stood the test, that person will receive the crown of life that the Lord has promised to those who love him" (James 1:12).

CHAPTER 10

A PLACE LIKE NO OTHER

THE IMAGE WILL stay with me for the rest of my life... An ocean of people from various tribes and tongues—numbering literally in the millions—worshipping the Lord, faces radiating His presence, arms uplifted, voices shouting, jumping, dancing, singing, praising; some with their faces on the ground, brought to their knees by the goodness of God.

The glory was so great in that open-air stadium in Nigeria, I was overcome. I just fell to my knees and cried and cried. Heaven had come to earth!

There is another image that remains in my mind's eye—this one from a short video highlighting clips from the 2014 international crusades of Reinhard Bonnke's and Daniel Kolenda's ministry, Christ for All Nations. Captured in a moment from Ibadan, Nigeria, was a wheelchair—no longer occupied, no longer needed—being passed above people's heads among rows of out-stretched hands, as if being carried down the river of God in the city of God (Rev. 22:1–2).

Both of these sights were a marvelous preview of the Christian's life to come.

Like an exciting movie trailer, God's Word previews His city and our future, whetting our desire for the real thing. And though what we're told is limited—with some of the details shrouded in prophetic language—three things can be concluded from what we *are* shown about heaven.

First, this is a place like no other place.

Second, we have so, so much to anticipate!

Best of all, its blessings will never end. Psalm 16:11 (NKJV) says, "At Your right hand are pleasures forevermore" (see also Dan. 12:2; 1 Pet. 1:4).

Worship will be there! Live music. People we've known, and ones we've always wanted to meet. Reunions will last forever, never again ending in another round of good-byes. Conversations will contain no tension or misunderstanding. Our labor will be sweet—wholly fulfilling and fun, with opportunities to express all of who we are and explore everything we were ever interested in. We will be surrounded by places to adventure in and beauty unimagined and love that knows no limits.

For every person who enters into eternal life, the finest and best things in this life are a mere shadow of all the glories that lie ahead. So whatever has been the richest meal to you on earth will be like tasteless water compared to the banquet food in heaven. Earth's most bedazzling jewel is heaven's coal. The most luxurious mansion you've seen? A hovel there.

And every aspect of the place will be characterized by joy. Unhindered, undisrupted joy (Ps. 16:11). All because the Lord dwells there and we will finally be in His presence.

Just try to imagine finally getting to be in the moment of the biggest and best experience you've ever had, with the One you've longed to spend it with . . . and enjoying it *undiminished*!

None of earth's grand events comes close to the magnificence of a single moment in heaven. In this life, not one ceremony or extravaganza ever takes place without something to taint it. The Super Bowl, Daytona, a major concert, Easter Sunday service, a presidential inauguration, a royal wedding, graduation day, Wimbledon, a milestone birthday party, the Masters, the Oscars—you name it. *If* you can even get a place on the guest list, there is always an obstructed view or a crowded seat. A bad back or aching knees. Rain or wind or cold. Hunger pangs. Distracting worries about the time or the office or the kids. Traffic delays and security concerns. Long lines. Rowdy children. And the sound levels are never *just right*.

But heaven? Profoundly perfect. Not one detail missed, not one moment lost or ruined.

What can we expect of this unprecedented place that has been prepared for God's own?

Pastor John Hagee has noted that "Saint Paul, the brilliant author of thirteen books of the New Testament, was given a guided tour of the celestial city. And when he put his pen to parchment, he still could not describe what God had prepared for those who love Him."[1] Paul was among the most educated men of his day, and yet all vocabulary failed him when viewing the brilliance and sheer elation of what will be.

We have far more words at our disposal than he or John (the writer of Revelation) did—more than one million in English alone, according to a 2014 estimate by the Global Language Monitor. And of those million-plus words, about 250,000 of them are adjectives. Yet when it comes to our life beyond, none of them—not one— is equal to the reality to come. Still, I like Randy Alcorn's take on it in his comprehensive study of the afterlife, *Heaven*: "Everything God tells us suggests we will look back at the present Earth and conclude, creatively speaking, that God was just 'warming up' and getting started."[2]

What's not to look forward to, if the best of this world is just a warmup? The truth is, we can't imagine it; it is inconceivable! But I also can't wait to live it!

Within the Bible's pages, certain details of the invisible world are announced, and its glory is opened to our view. Many additional realities are indicated, even if not directly told. Rather than gazing through pinholes in the curtain that divides this life from the next, the biblical accounts actually part the veil and allow us to see, off in the distance, a landscape, a horizon, a city in another world. The one that will someday be ours.

THOSE WHO DIE IN CHRIST BEFORE HE RETURNS TO CARRY OUT HIS FINAL JUDGMENT ENTER PARADISE.

Jesus assured the thief on the cross, "Today you will be with me in paradise" (Luke 23:43). Paul was "caught up into paradise," which he also called "the third heaven," and shown "things that cannot be told" (2 Cor. 12:2–4 ESV). This present heaven is a beautiful place of rest for the spirits of the redeemed until they are given their resurrected bodies and take occupancy of the new heaven and earth.

When I say "rest," don't think "sleep and laziness"; think "rest," as in relief from the problems and fears and pains of earth. This paradise is also a holy home, free of sin and its effects, like the original Eden was.

As Christ triumphs once and for all over His foes, and the new heaven and earth are established, the redeemed will receive the fulfillment of all that they've been promised.

While they await these blessed events, our loved ones who have entered eternal life are reunited with one another and face-to-face with God. They know true joy and comfort, communion and worship. They understand (and possibly see) what they could not when confined by the limits of life below. And with this knowledge, believe some pastors and theologians, they intercede on our behalf.

When I study the context between the poor man, Lazarus, and the rich man in Luke 16, this conclusion has merit. Both men had died and passed into eternity—Lazarus to the peace and comfort of Paradise and the rich man to the agony of Hades' flames. Though there was a "great gulf [or "chasm," per NASB] fixed" between them that could not be crossed (v. 26 NKJV), Father Abraham (whom Lazarus was with) and the rich man were still able to see and speak to each other. And the one in Hades was concerned that his brothers who survived him were still unsaved.

Maybe he only knew they weren't yet with him in Hades, and thus he assumed they were still on earth and unsaved. Maybe he was basing his concerns on what he now experienced of eternity and what he'd known of their unrepentance on earth. But it is also possible that the inhabitants of the present heaven and hell are somehow aware of what happens on earth and the status of their loved ones.

Some pastors who I highly respect believe that the "cloud of witnesses" mentioned in Hebrews 12:1–3 doesn't mean those who have preceded us into eternity are watching us and cheering us on directly, but rather that their biblical testimonies of faithfulness should inspire our own.[3] Other theologians whom I also respect conclude from the biblical record that the faithful in Paradise are praying for us who are still on our earthly way. "These sainted millions have run their race..." explained Pastor John Rice; "They have finished their course. Now they watch... as we take our places."[4]

"Did you hear that...?" encouraged J. Sidlow Baxter. "Your treasured one yonder is thinking of you, loving you... *praying* for you with such enlightened understanding that every such intercession is answered with a divine 'Yes.'"[5]

When I think of Chad alongside Jesus, possibly interceding for Deborah and Christian and me as we journey toward our true home, it comforts me like almost nothing else. Whether he is aware of our earthly state or not, however, I know this without a doubt: he is in the presence of God and enjoying the sweet rest of Paradise (Ps. 73:25; 2 Cor. 5:8). Because of this, I have the comfort of knowing he is safe, he is healed, and he is happier than he has ever been.

ONE DAY THERE WILL BE A NEW WORLD CONTAINING AN EVERLASTING CITY—AND THIS WILL BE OUR ETERNAL HOME.

That world will be a real place, as earth is, with dimension and texture and a distinct environment. And in its midst will be a real city like Tokyo, Paris, or Los Angeles—only permanent, infinite . . . and perfect (Dan. 2:44; Isa. 9:7; Heb. 11:16). Everything that represents "home" to us—everything that matters here—will be present there, yet "as different as a real thing is from a shadow or as waking life is from a dream."[6] In that day, we will discover that what seems the substance now will prove to have been the dream. Heaven is the real; earth is the shadow.

Scripture calls that place "the city which has foundations, whose builder and maker is God" (Heb. 11:10 NKJV). It is full of magnificent estates custom-made for each of its citizens (1 Cor. 2:9, 10), and it will never pass away (Dan. 7:14).

According to Bishop Keith Butler, "If you want to see what Heaven is like—its design—picture the earth without decay or sin," and with far more of everything good and beautiful and breathtaking and pure. "The beauty of the earth is not in the same league," he says, "yet it is in God's taste, because He created it."[7] In fact, says the Unicorn in the final book of the Chronicles of Narnia, "The reason why we loved the old Narnia is that it sometimes looked a little like this [the new Narnia]."[8]

The New Jerusalem will reside on a new earth (Rev. 21:1–3) and be indescribably lavish—with jewels and gold and gemstones as its construction materials rather than the steel and stone and wood of earth. It will have twelve foundations—what Dr. David Jeremiah surmises are probably twelve layers surrounding it—and twelve gates, each one made of a single pearl and guarded by an angel to prevent evil influences and intruders (Rev. 21:18–21). Pastor John MacArthur believes the pearls will not be "from some giant variety of oysters, but perfect pearls created by God's own hand."[9] These gates will never be shut (Rev. 21:12)—the citizens of this Jerusalem are free to roam the city and beyond.

The New Jerusalem will be an enormous, uniform cube, as high and wide as it is long (Rev. 21:16). Why a cube? MacArthur reminds us that the Holy of Holies in Solomon's Temple was also a cube, though on a much smaller scale (1 Kgs. 6:20): "The New Jerusalem is the Holy of Holies for eternity . . . the very sanctuary of God Himself."[10]

Tallying up the literal, biblical measurements, the blessed city's total area of coverage—1,400 or 1,500 square miles high (depending on the Bible translation you reference) and some two million square miles on the ground—would be over three billion cubic miles. By contrast, New York City's land area is a mere 305 square miles.

How many people will three billion-plus cubic miles hold? The foremost answer is: "As many as received Him" and became "children of God" (John 1:12 NKJV). Statistically speaking, "even if everyone who ever lived was saved [approximately thirty billion people]," figures Pastor Steven J. Lawson, "that would still allow each person 200 square miles on the ground alone . . . And that's just in the city!"[11]

All told, heaven could house one hundred thousand *hundred billion* citizens!

The city will be surrounded by a thick, glimmering jasper wall. This is not a barrier; there's no need for one, since all enemies and their threat of attack will be gone. Instead, it probably serves to define the city's borders. Main Street and the city itself will be made of pure gold, but far finer than what we're used to. Heaven's version will be transparent, like glass (Rev. 21:18, 21).

The biblical writers give us further introduction to life within this heavenly city[12]:

- It houses God's throne. David said: "I lift up my eyes to you, to you who sit enthroned in heaven" (Ps. 123:1). Micaiah "saw the LORD sitting on his throne with all the multitudes of heaven standing on his right and on his left" (2 Chron. 18:18). John "saw a throne in heaven" and "the one sitting on [it] was as brilliant as gemstones—like jasper and carnelian. And the glow of an emerald circled his throne like a rainbow" with two dozen other thrones—those of the elders of Revelation—surrounding God's. "From the throne came flashes of lightning and the rumble of thunder" (Rev. 4:2–5 NLT).

- Representatives from the tribes and nations of the earth will all be there, as well as the twelve apostles and the twelve tribes of Israel (Rev. 7:4–10; 21:12, 14, 24). According to Wikipedia, New York City is the most linguistically diverse city in the world, with an estimated eight hundred languages spoken there. Heaven will be home to even more tongues.

- Its natural wonders will include waters and parks and trees with healing properties. John was shown "a shiny sea of glass, sparkling like crystal" (Rev. 4:6 NLT) in front of God's throne and "a river with the water of life, clear as crystal, flowing from the throne of God and of the Lamb . . . down the center of the main street" (Rev. 22:1–2 NLT). The river of God is one that the psalmist wrote about: "There is a river, the streams whereof shall make glad the city of God" (Ps. 46:4 KJV). "On each side of the river grew a tree of life, bearing twelve crops of fruit, with a fresh crop each month. The leaves were used for medicine to heal the nations" (Rev. 22:2 NLT). According to William Hendriksen, in the original language, this "tree of life" entails not just one tree but many—a park's worth, right in the heart of Paradise (Rev. 2:7).[13] Heaven's inhabitants will be allowed to eat the fruit from such a tree (Rev. 22:14). The setting echoes Eden (Gen. 2:9–10), only better.

- There will be music and celebration, singing and worship—and certainly even some dancing in honor to the Lord: "The ransomed of the LORD will return. They will enter Zion with singing; everlasting joy will crown their heads. Gladness and joy will overtake them, and sorrow and sighing will flee away" (Isa. 35:10; see also Rev. 5:8–9, 11–14; 14:2–3; 15:2–4). Revelation 14:3 speaks of "a great choir" (NLT). There are several mentions of harps and trumpets specifically in Revelation, but considering the variety of instruments that accompanied war and worship and celebration in biblical times, we can safely anticipate additional sounds of music in the new kingdom.

- There's no darkness, no sun, moon, or stars, for God's glory illuminates it with the brilliance of a precious jewel—like a diamond perhaps?—and "the Lamb is its light" (Rev. 21:11, 22–25).

- There is "no night there—no need for lamps or sun—for the Lord God will shine on them" (Rev. 22:5).

- Peter wrote that righteousness will inhabit the new earth (2 Peter 3:13). So this is a place with no war—no factions, denominations, or angry debates. All will be one with Jesus, the Prince of Peace, and aware that true power belongs to God (Isa. 62:1–2).

- There's no more curse in heaven. Think about it. Every byproduct of the Fall will no longer exist (Rev. 22:3). Everyone is fully satisfied, content. And with evil defeated, this city will experience no corruption, no idol worship or immorality; it will not have to suffer con men and their deceptions . . . or criminals and the fear they provoke (Rev. 20:10; 21:8, 27). The absence of sin means that nothing entering heaven will defile, contaminate, or pollute the land or its inhabitants. Everything in heaven reflects the perfection of God (Rev. 21:27).

THIS HEAVENLY WORLD WILL BE INHABITED.

- *God is present in the heavenly realm.* He dwells as a Father with His children, as a King amid His subjects (Ps. 16:11, Ps. 123:1, Luke 11:2). The great evangelist Jonathan Edwards preached: "Heaven is the . . . Father's house . . . It is the place of the Most

High God; it is the place where God is gloriously present... where God is to be seen, where He is to be enjoyed, where His love is graciously manifested... and [the godly man sees Him] as He is, where he may love, praise, and enjoy Him perfectly."[14]

- *Jesus is there.* When Jesus ascended into heaven, He took His seat at the right hand of the Father (John 17:24; Acts 1:9–11). John's vision of Him there was as a slain Lamb reconciling transgressors to God and also as the conquering King (Rev. 5:6; 19:11–16). Paul referred to Him as the head and worship of all things "in heaven and on earth and under the earth" (Phil. 2:9–11; see also Rev. 5:6–12), including the church, the redeemed of the Lord (Eph. 1:20–23).

- *Angels are in heaven.* The "elect" angels—those who did not rebel against God before time—number "ten thousand times ten thousand, and thousands of thousands" (Rev. 5:11–12 NKJV; also see Heb. 12:22), which in scriptural terms means a number without measure. They live in the presence of God (Ps. 148:2; Matt. 18:10; Rev. 3:5; 8:2–3) and are witnesses to and participants in all the proceedings of heaven (Rev. 7:1; 14:10; 18:21; 19:17). Both the Old Testament and the New are packed with accounts of angels appearing from on high with messages for the residents of earth, or to rescue or minister, or to dispense God's judgment (Gen. 16:7–13; Num. 22:35; Judg. 6:12; 13:2–6; 1 Kgs. 19:5–8; Ps. 103:20; Dan. 3:19–28; 10:13; Zech. 1:10–11; Matt. 28:2, 5; Luke 1:13, 19, 26; 2:10–15; Acts 5:17–20; 2 Thess. 1:7; Heb. 1:14; Rev. 9:14–15; 14:17–20; 15:1). They carry us away to heaven when we die (Luke 16:22). They are also heaven's warriors and will accompany Jesus when He comes again (Matt. 25:31; Rev. 12:7; 20:1–3). Joni Eareckson Tada, in her book *Heaven... Your Real Home,* believes that we will know the angels by name and fellowship with them personally. We will most certainly worship God alongside them (Ps. 103:21; Ps. 148:2; Rev. 7:11–12). And per their assigned responsibilities, they will serve us in heaven (Heb. 1:14).[15]

- *The Holy Spirit will be there.* Among His many roles on earth, the Holy Spirit is God's restraining force against the full powers of evil until Jesus returns. At the Rapture, the Spirit will be removed and will permanently resume residence in heaven (2 Thess. 2:7–8; Rev. 4:5). John described the Spirit of God as seven burning torches in front of the throne (Rev. 4:5 NLT) and later was privy to this conversation in his prophetic vision: "Then I heard a voice from heaven say, 'Write this: Blessed are the dead who die in the Lord from now on.' 'Yes,' says the Spirit, 'they will rest from their labor, for their deeds will follow them'" (Rev. 14:13 NLT).

- *The righteous—Christ's bride, the church—will dwell there.* At the Rapture, all the dead in Christ, and any believers living at that time, will be "caught up together... to meet the Lord in the air" (1 Thess. 4:16–17). This is when all the saints of God will receive their glorified bodies: "Your dead will live, LORD; their bodies will rise—let those who dwell in the dust wake up and shout for joy" (Isa. 26:19). His beloved will also return with Him to earth at His second coming to celebrate the wedding feast (Rev. 19:7–8, 14; 21:9–11). God's people will remain in His presence forevermore (Job 19:26–27; 1 Thess. 4:17; Rev. 22:3–4) and rule with Christ over both the new heaven and new earth (Dan. 7:18, 27; Rev. 3:21). Revelation 5:10 says: "You have made them to be a kingdom and priests to serve our God, and they will reign on the earth"—the new earth, that is.

- *Twenty-four elders "all clothed in white" and wearing gold crowns will be there* (Rev. 4:4 NLT), and they will be joined by the four beasts around the throne (Rev. 4:6–8) and the Jewish converts from the Tribulation who took the seal of the Lord rather than the mark of the Beast (Matt. 14:14; 28:19–20; Rev. 7:3–8; 14:1).

- *Animals will be there.* The majority of scholars believe that, as in

Eden, animals will be in heaven (Ps. 148:10–13). Scripture not only speaks of predator and prey existing harmoniously there (Isa. 11:6–8; 65:25) but mentions horses and other creatures.

In light of all these things, we need not doubt the reality of this great and future city, or how good it will be to live there. Even more intriguing is what *we* will be like! I have covered this in the next chapter.

CHAPTER 11

FOREVER CHANGED

FIRST CORINTHIANS 15:52 captures one of the most memorable moments in Scripture: "In a flash, in the twinkling of an eye...the trumpet will sound, the dead will be raised imperishable, and we [who are living] will be changed." What will change? How will *we* be changed?

The Message explains it this way: "On signal from that trumpet from heaven, the dead will be up and out of their graves, beyond the reach of death, never to die again. At the same moment and in the same way, we'll all be changed. In the resurrection scheme of things, this has to happen: everything perishable taken off the shelves and replaced by the imperishable, this mortal replaced by the immortal."

Much about our lives will whisper of the familiar once we are all united with our resurrected bodies and the entire family of God in heaven. Yet all will be different. Transformed. Glorified. Magnified. Amplified. Heightened.

WHAT HAS BEEN WILL BE GLORIOUSLY CHANGED.
The curse will be removed (Rev. 22:3)! And with it, all will be made new (Rev. 21:5). Richard Baxter exulted that, come heaven, we will have "changed our place and state, our clothes and thoughts, our look, language, and company."[1]

We will have resurrected bodies and minds—enhanced, improved, perfected...thoroughly healed (Isa. 35:5). What every doctor dreams of! It will be a spiritual body. Not just *spirit*, like wispy clouds or ghostly apparitions, but *spiritual*, immortal, eternal—just like our souls. "If there is a natural body, there is also a spiritual body," Paul said (1 Cor. 15:44). "We know that if the earthly tent we live in is destroyed, we have a building from God, an eternal house in heaven, not built by human hands" (2 Cor. 5:1).

What will that glorious body be like? We can have some idea by studying our earthly form. "Somewhere in my broken, paralyzed body is the seed of what I shall become," Joni Eareckson Tada has written.[2]

Jill Briscoe admits: "Some of us that have struggled with accepting the bodies we have been given for earth may not be terribly enthralled with the idea of another one quite like it for eternity!" But she reminds us that Paul pictured our heavenly and earthly forms as different as a blossom to the bulb. "Think of a daffodil bulb," Briscoe urges. "Then think of the flower. Could there be any comparison between them? Yet both are unmistakably daffodil in nature." Both are suited for their environment, she continues: "One belongs to the earth...But the flower of the bulb dances in the fresh air and sunlight about the ground."[4]

Here's another way of understanding the difference:

This image of planting a dead seed and raising a live plant is a mere sketch at best, but perhaps it will help in approaching the mystery of the resurrection body—but only if you keep in mind that when we're raised, we're raised for *good*, alive forever! The corpse that's planted is no beauty, but when it's raised, it's glorious. Put in the ground weak, it comes up powerful. The seed sown is natural; the seed grown is supernatural—same seed, same body, but what a difference from when it goes down in physical mortality to when it is raised up in spiritual immortality! (1 Cor. 15:42–44 MSG)

"Bible Answer Man" and president of the Christian Research Institute, Hank Hanegraaff, explains: "Our eternal bodies are numerically identical to the bodies we now possess. As Christ rose in the same physical body in which he died, so too we will be raised in the same physical body in which we die. In other words, our resurrection body is not a second temporary body; rather it is our present body transformed (1 Cor. 15:42–43)."[4]

According to Paul, what was once perishing and perishable, dishonorable, and weak in its physical form becomes indestructible, glorified, and powerful in its spiritual form, perfectly suited for life in heaven 2 Cor. 5:1–5). Just as we bear the image of the first man, Adam, and his dusty-earth form in our humanity, we bear the image of heaven and the "heavenly man," Jesus, in the afterlife (1 Cor. 15:47–49).

Our better bodies will have shape and substance yet will be able to move about instantly and freely, just like Jesus could after His resurrection. We will *not* resemble the angels; we will look like ourselves, but without flaw. This means that those who knew us on earth will recognize us in our eternal form, though we may not look the age at which we died. Especially for those who died very young or very old, asserts Hanegraaff, we can reasonably expect them to be "resurrected physically mature" based on the fact that Adam and Eve were created as adults in the perfection of Eden.[5]

The resurrected Jesus gives us further clues about what our glorified bodies will be like. He was not just spirit; He could be touched (Luke 24:39; John 20:27), He walked and talked with people on earth (Luke 24; Acts 1:3), and He ate with them (John 21:12–15; Acts 1:4–5). He was different enough in appearance that those who knew Him didn't always recognize Him at first—such as Mary at the tomb—but once He spoke to them, they realized it was Him.

Hanegraaff, appealing to both science and the Bible, has concluded that "if the blueprint for our glorified bodies is in the DNA, then it would stand to reason that our bodies will be resurrected at the optimal stage of development determined by our DNA."[6]

EVERYTHING WRONG ON EARTH WILL BE MADE UTTERLY RIGHT.

One way to think of this is that when we are finally with the Lord in His kingdom, nothing will be broken anymore. Not our bodies or our minds or our hearts. Not our families or our wills. We will have rest from temptation and the accusations of the devil; we will no longer fight the lusts and addictions of the flesh. All fear will be vanquished, all dreams and hopes and godly desires fulfilled. Every single thing will be set straight and purified.

With our new bodies and minds will come wholesome desires (1 John 3:2). What we long for and enjoy will be untainted, right, and good. Every thought in the heavenly world will be holy and pleasing to God; every deed a tribute to Him (Rev. 21:27). We will no longer sin, no longer be sinners, no longer be enslaved by our own sin or that of others.

Everything about us—including our ability to love and be loved—will be able to operate at full capacity. This can happen in a world where there is no sin.

Of his heaven-and-back experience after a plane crash, pilot Dale Black said: "The absence of sin was something you could feel. There was no shame because there was nothing to be ashamed of. There was no sadness, because there was nothing to be sad about. There was no need to hide, because there was nothing to hide from. It was all out in the open. Clean and pure. Here was perfection."[7]

There is no death in heaven (Dan. 12:2; Luke 20:36; Rev. 1:18; 19:11; 21:4). Justice will be done; sin will be purged and punished; death will be no longer. No sufferings or sorrows will reach us there either. God will wipe away every tear (Isa. 65:19; Rev. 7:17; 21:4). Charles Spurgeon said, "In heaven our joy will be full, without mixture of sorrow (John 16:20). Then there will be no sorrow for a present trouble, nor present fear of future troubles."[8] D. L. Moody described it this way: "In heaven there is all life and no death. In hell there is all death and no life."[9] Put another way, in heaven we will be restored and able to live to the full (Isa. 35:5–6; 1 Cor. 15:35–58; 2 Cor. 5:1–9; Rev. 21:3–7). Our bodies cannot be subjected to pain or disease in that place (Phil. 3:20–21). And we will never have to be absent from the ones we love again. Not for a moment! "Endings" will be no more!

"Tears are only for earth," commented Herbert Lockyer.[10] So are farewells. There will be no want in the heavenly world, no lack of anything that may be necessary to make its inhabitants happy (Rev. 7:16). And "relationship" and "fellowship" are two of those necessities.

We know all about endings from earth's side of eternity. Even happy endings are still . . . endings—and therefore bittersweet. But even though believers are disappearing from this world one by one, says Randy Alcorn, and those of us who remain here are saddened that they have "left home, in reality . . . our believing loved ones aren't leaving home, they're going home. They'll be home before us. We'll be arriving at the party a little later. Laughing and rejoicing—a party awaits us."[11]

Missing Chad as much as I still do, I cling to the truth of Jesus' words in John 16:22, for what was true of that reunion with Him will be true of our reunion with the friends and family we have loved: "Now is your time of grief, but I will see you again and you will rejoice, and no one will take away your joy."

WE WILL BE FULLY, GLORIOUSLY, JOYOUSLY OCCUPIED.
This question of "What will we do there for years upon years of eternity?" may be one of the most asked and misunderstood concerns of all.

Lutzer and others assure us that we will not suddenly lose our identities—all those things that make us unique. Our personal knowledge, interests, personalities, and relationships with other believers and the Lord will continue into heaven, and we will continue to grow in our thinking and talents.[12]

Heaven will be a constantly expanding place—perfect not only for the pursuits of work but the enjoyment of play. Nothing will turn stale. Our every experience will be a dynamic, ever-engaging discovery that leads us to the next new thing.

The world to come will contain endless possibilities for adventure, exploration, creativity, and anything that fascinates. Mark Buchanan anticipates it as a meeting of "the *ahh!* of deep satisfaction and the *aha!* of delighted surprise."[13]

We will not leave behind our imaginations either—they will be inspired to new heights and depths as we assist God in developing and shaping the new earth. So whether you love to sing, or build, or design, or experiment, or choreograph, or create, get ready: your passions will have a place to be expressed, and the possibilities will only multiply the longer you're there.

"Even under the Curse, human imagination and skill have produced some remarkable works," writes Alcorn. "Stonehenge. Shakespeare's plays. Beethoven's Ninth Symphony. The Golden Gate Bridge. Baseball. Heart transplants...The space shuttle... Pecan pie. Sports cars...With the resources God will lavishly give us on the New Earth, what will we be able to accomplish together? When we think about this, we should be like children anticipating Christmas—sneaking out of bed to see what's under the Christmas tree."[14]

Boredom is one thing that Christians worry about in heaven, but this is not what biblical "rest" means (Heb. 4:9; Rev. 14:13)! The sons and daughters of God will have rest from what makes work "labor"—the toil and heat and sweat and stress that was introduced by the curse in Eden. We will still, however, enjoy all the rewards and fulfillment of whatever it is that we love to do. We will no longer have to provide our own food, for example, or put a roof over our own heads. However, the current consensus among Christian thinkers seems to be that if we love those things in this life, we will not be deprived of them in a perfect world. Rather, we will have both the endless resources and opportunities to continue our craft, whether we farm heaven's fields or prepare heaven's banquets or develop its land.

The hardness and uncertainty that plague our labors on earth will be replaced by goodness and joy and gratification (Matt. 25:22–23; Rev. 22:3). In the New International Version, the last sentence of Isaiah 35:10 reads: "Gladness and joy will overtake them, and sorrow and sighing will flee away." You won't just be happy in heaven; you'll be elated! You won't just enjoy your work; you'll be completely absorbed by it, never tiring of it or getting tired by it!

There will be no sighing in exhaustion or frustration. No wasted energy. No lost time. No disappointing results. If we plant and tend a seed, it will flourish. If we take the time to build a wall, it will be plumb. If we sew a hem, it will be straight and true. If we dance, we will hit our marks. We will truly be able to work with all our heart unto the Lord (Col. 3:23), without disruptions or delays, micromanaging bosses or harsh instructors. And we will reap a harvest for our efforts.

Most of all, our work will have a purpose in heaven: service (Rev. 7:15). Life and glad obedience go hand in hand there. We will rule and reign forever as kings and priests to our God (Rev. 2:26). We will honor Him with the work of our hands and hearts and minds, and worship Him without hindrance, obstacle, or hassle—forever (Rev. 22:5). What a day that will be!

WE WILL BE HOME AT LAST.
"The heaven of fact exists all glorious and enduring," said E. M. Bounds, "but this fact of heaven must enter our experience, and then of this experience hope is born."[15]

Heaven is a place like no other, with mysteries and glories untold but waiting to captivate our every sense. It is what anchors our hope throughout this life and spurs us in the next. Of all that it is, though, and all that it offers, what is its most important aspect? David Jeremiah tells us:

Sometimes heaven is referred to as a country, and we think of its vastness. Sometimes heaven is referred to as a city, and we think of its inhabitants. Sometimes heaven is called a kingdom, and we think of its orderliness. Sometimes heaven is called Paradise, and we imagine its beauty. But when we call heaven the Father's house, we think of intimacy and permanency. The most important feature of this New Jerusalem is that God and the Lamb will be there, forever![16]

And where they are, we also shall be. Finally in heaven. Finally home.

PART III
THY KINGDOM COME

CHAPTER 12
A LIVING HOPE

EVERYTHING I'VE READ and heard regarding the realities of heaven impassions me for my destiny. The more I learn, the more I long to get there. Yet plenty of Christians have been accused of being "so heavenly minded" that they are "of no earthly good."

Heaven isn't only what will be. It's not only the there-and-back experiences when people glimpse eternity themselves, or those reach-across-the-divide moments when the supernatural intervenes in our natural world and outright miracles or deliverances take place. There is another aspect of heaven we must understand as well: God's eternal kingdom here on earth, here among us.

This is the piece of heaven that every believer has daily exposure to. It's the element of heaven that Jesus prayed for and invited His followers to operate in ("Thy kingdom come, Thy will be done in earth, as it is in heaven," Matt. 6:10 KJV). It's the realm where I try to live out my life until my heavenly Father calls me home.

The kingdom of heaven come to earth is on display in many forms, but I can pinpoint four significant ways it reveals itself every day in my life and the life of every child of God who has eternity in view: no fear of evil, all-surpassing peace and comfort, salvation and personal transformation, and a commissioning fire to reach the lost.

I want to speak to each of these in the closing chapters of this book, because they are Christ's gifts for everyone who believes, to carry us across the finish line of this life.

HOPE WITHOUT FEAR

Rather than "fearless hope," which is the birthright of every child of God, a lot of people—even longtime Christians—have "fearful hope." They believe God *can* heal, deliver, and save, and they know He does sometimes...but *will He* show up when they need Him? They hope so; they beg for Him to; but deep down, they're afraid He simply won't.

I get it. I've been guilty of this myself. In reality, though, fearful hope is nothing more than wishful thinking. And mere wishful thinking is not the stuff of faith.

In *A Grief Observed*, C. S. Lewis wrote: "You never know how much you really believe anything until its truth or falsehood becomes a matter of life and death to you. It is easy to say you believe a rope to be strong and sound as long as you are merely using it to cord a box. But suppose you had to hang by that rope over a precipice. Wouldn't you then first discover how much you really trusted it?"[1]

Our most desolate hours prove whether our faith rests in the rock-solid promises of God or the whims of this world. Whether our hope is in the goodness of God or the ability of man.

Hank Hanegraaff calls faith "a channel of living trust—an assurance—that stretches from man to God...that God's promises will never fail, even if sometimes we do not experience their fulfillment in our mortal [earthly] existence."[2] Faith's companion, hope, looks with anticipation to that day when those promises will be fulfilled.

Martin Luther wrote that hope both "fight[s] against...heaviness of spirit, weakness, despair, and blasphemy" and "waits for good things even in the midst of all evils." It stirs the mind to courage, enabling God's people to "endure adversity" while they "wait for better things."[3] I like that. Christians don't just wish for better things; we wait for them, confident they are coming.

In addition, in those same pages in his commentary on Galatians, Luther described God's truth as the object of faith, and God's goodness as the object of hope. The truth of faith helps us battle the enemy's lies, while the confidence of hope helps us counter Satan's assaults on our weaknesses and emotions. When he tries to deceive, we hold up the shield of faith to "extinguish all the flaming arrows of the evil one" (Eph. 6:16). When he preys on our vulnerabilities, attempting to discourage or frighten or make us impatient, we engage our hope and continue to reinforce it with the reliability of God's promises.

In other words, biblical hope plans on and expects that God will be true to His word and good to His people. Biblical faith knows that He is.

ON FIRM GROUND

The Lord's enduring faithfulness and goodness are not just reserved for our future in heaven; they are the two legs Christians can stand on in this life when everything seems to be collapsing around them. Psalm 23:4–6 says as much: "Though I walk through the valley of the shadow of death, I will fear no evil; for You are with me; Your rod and Your staff, they comfort me. You prepare a table before me in the presence of my enemies; You anoint my head with oil; my cup runs over. Surely goodness and mercy shall follow me all the days of my life; and I will dwell in the house of the LORD forever" (NKJV).

"Why would God have us walk through danger to get to him?" asks Christian psychologist Dan Allender. "Valleys strip us of the presumption of independence; danger draws us to greater dependence on the only one who can provide and protect. The desert brings us to our knees with craving; the valley calls us to cling to the hem of the one who waits us to safety."[4]

That God's kingdom has come means His sons and daughters

carry the surety of heaven's promise in their hearts as they make their way toward home. So when the enemy tries to flood us with fearful weather (such as the whirlwind of cancer), we "hold unswervingly to the hope we profess, for he who promised is faithful" (Heb. 10:23). The storm may continue to rage for a time—the specter of death may stand over us—but we are no longer cowered by our surroundings; the Rock on which we stand is permanent. Fixed. Everlasting. We see earthly threats for what they are. And in the light of eternity, death has no more substance than a shadow.

In the land of living hope—in this bold frontier that Jesus has claimed for every believer—the threats of earth lose their power to intimidate because we've learned: these too shall pass. The things of earth lose their hold because this world is not our home. We fear no evil and no enemy because our God is greater.

To find oneself in that secure territory is an enormous turning point for any child of God.

Recently an elderly woman arrested on our medical floor, with no blood pressure or heart rate. Our code team responded with CPR and life-support measures, and those measures successfully resuscitated her. Afterward, she told me she felt the presence of God in the room while she was being worked on, and in His presence was pervasive peace. She also reported seeing Jesus standing above the doctors and nurses as they worked. Jesus was reaching toward her with His hands extended and His palms up. He was dressed in white but she did not see His face.

Mrs. Humphries excitedly called everyone in her family and told them about her encounter with Jesus. But what made the biggest impression on me is what remained with her: after that incident she told me, "I'm no longer afraid to die."

Several years ago, a patient of ours at Palm Beach Gardens Medical Center had a similar outcome. Ms. Sharon told me that while she was being resuscitated, she felt as if she was pushing through a crowd of people and past an array of curtains until she heard the Lord tell her to stand down: "It isn't your time yet." She was very emotional as she relayed the story to me, pausing through many tears to gather herself. "No one can tell me it wasn't real— that I wasn't almost home," she declared with fortitude. "Because I know I was."

I think the surest sign of a living hope—a hope that fears no evil—is in the Christian's ability to "be still and know" that the Lord is God (Ps. 46:10) and that His "love stands firm forever," His faithfulness "established...in heaven itself" (Ps. 89:2). Hebrews 6 speaks of the hope laid out before us by our promise-keeping God, who cannot lie. "This hope we have as an anchor of the soul...both sure and steadfast," says verse 19 (NASB).

We Christians have faith and real expectation, right now, that heaven awaits because Christ died and returned to life. He did this, says Romans 14:9, "so that he might be the Lord of both the dead and the living." Thanks to Him, we can walk through our days assured that "if we live, we live for the Lord; and if we die, we die for the Lord. So, whether we live or die, we belong to the Lord" (Rom. 14:8).

The resurrection of Christ is crucial to more than faith; it is the source of Christian hope. The apostle Paul said, "If Christ has not been raised [from the dead], our preaching is useless and so is your faith," because "those also who have fallen asleep in Christ are lost. If only for this life we have hope in Christ, we are of all people most to be pitied" (1 Cor. 15:14, 18–19). Elaborating further, he said, "What's the point of endangering ourselves every hour and facing death every day if we have no living hope?" Christians in biblical times—much like in other parts of the world today—risked their lives to even affirm the gospel. To actually travel to the corners of the world and share it, as Paul and his cohorts were doing (and as today's missionaries and evangelists do), was lunacy if there was no eternal reality behind it. "If I fought wild beasts in Ephesus with no more than human hopes," he argued, "what have I gained? If the dead are

not raised, [then] 'Let us eat and drink, for tomorrow we die.'"
(1 Cor. 15:30–32).

Thankfully, neither faith nor the hope of the Christian is futile.
I love what Jeremiah 17:7–9 promises: "Blessed is the one who
trusts in the LORD, whose confidence is in him. They will be like
a tree planted by the water that sends out its roots by the stream. It
does not fear when heat comes; its leaves are always green. It has
no worries in a year of drought and never fails to bear fruit."

Scripture declares that the Lord alone is to be feared. As long as
we reverently respect and position ourselves under Him, we need
not fear anything else. God exhorts us, "Do not fear..."

- when destruction comes (Job 5:21).
- though you are attacked from every angle (Ps. 3:6).
- though an army besiege you and war break out against you (Ps. 27:3).
- though the earth collapse and the mountains fall into the sea (Ps. 46:2).
- the terror of night or the enemy's arrows (Ps. 91:5).
- harm or disaster (Ps. 91:10).
- the reproach or insults of others (Isa. 51:7).
- disgrace, humiliation, or shame from your past (Isa. 54:4).
- those who can kill the body but not the soul (Matt. 10:28).
- the threats of those who seek to harm you (1 Pet. 3:14).

Not even the evil one himself should hold any sway over us (1
John 5:18).

Maybe people aren't that afraid of Satan anymore; I don't know.
But the one thing that unsettles nearly everyone is the threat of
death. I see it every day in my line of work. Of all the weapons of
the evil one, the threat of death is his nuclear device—his weapon
of mass destruction. With it, he decimates anything that is not
grounded in the truth and goodness of God.

STARING DOWN A GUN BARREL

Being able to fearlessly look death in the eye with hope intact is the true test of faith. Three Jewish youths in ancient Babylon—Shadrach, Meshach, and Abednego—stood firm even when threatened with the fiery furnace, declaring to the king: "Our God whom we serve is able to deliver us from the furnace of blazing fire…But *even if He does not*, let it be known to you, O king, that we are not going to serve your gods" (Dan. 3:17–18 NASB).

Whether out of the fire or through it, God delivers those who trust in Him. And as Halloween of 2004 approached, my family and I were about to be tested as never before.

The morning that Deborah prayed our son Chad back to life was a few days before Halloween. She had anointed him with oil and piped in praise music with headphones on his ears so that his spirit could worship even if his body wasn't responding. That's when she started to see a mist around him—the glory of God's presence. It continued as long as there was worship and prayer. When she would stop, the mist seemed to disappear.

At one point, Chad raised his hands to heaven. Our reserved fifteen-year-old son, who was too self-conscious to ever raise his hands in church, *held up his hands*! Deborah believes he was probably between heaven and earth then.

On the eve of Halloween, Chad declined again. In many ways, it seemed we were fighting a losing battle. Not only was our son struggling, but it didn't escape our notice that most of the hospital staff was dressed like the darkness—from witches to goblins to monsters and frightful beasts. Nevertheless, Deborah continued speaking God's Word over him.

She and Christian and I spent the night at his bedside. On Halloween Day, we got a call from our dear friend Larry Stockstill, who suggested we gather around Chad and place him in God's hands. With the three of us surrounding Chad's bed, we grasped hands over him and asked the Lord to accomplish His will. It was still our belief, however, that God intended to heal our boy.

We all stayed with him through the evening, though well after Christian and I fell asleep, Deborah remained on the night watch, praying. There came a point when she sensed the Lord speaking to her, and it was as straightforward as could be: "If you will lift your praises to Me, you will activate the armies of the living God."

My wife was quick to respond—and she kept on for several hours. Chad did too, in his own way: as long as his mother remained in praise and stayed awake, his heart rate and vital signs were stable.

However, both Deborah and the nurse on duty that night noticed that whenever Deborah would stop or her worship was interrupted for any reason, Chad's heart rate and vital signs would drop. As soon as his mother would start up again, Chad's vitals would rebound. It was so much like the account in Exodus 17 where, as long as Moses' arms were lifted up, Israel's army would gain the edge in the battle, but if his arms dropped, the Israelites would begin to lose.

The nurse told her not to stop. Deborah kept on with her prayer-and-praise vigil until she fell asleep briefly, around three thirty a.m., and then she picked up again twenty minutes later. Finally, she fell asleep for good and awoke a few hours later to the sound of the alarms on the monitors.

It was the day after Halloween, November 1, which is All Saints' Day—the mist was there, the glory of God's presence. Chad survived the night, but barely.

The dawn greeted us with clear skies. It was a gorgeous morning in Houston—not a cloud in sight, beautiful blue overhead everywhere we looked. Though it's impossible to know what any day will hold when a loved one is in intensive care, fighting for their life, I couldn't help but think that if the sky was any predictor, Chad might have a decent day.

My son, however, wasn't breathing well.

What's more, as I gazed out the window of his hospital room mid-morning, I spied a tiny black cloud on the blue horizon. As it got closer, I could see lightning coming out of it. Then I noticed blackbirds gathered in the foliage beneath his window. When the approaching cloud of glory thundered and flashed with lightning, the birds scattered. The lightning was so strong that our phone connection with a missionary friend in Mexico kept getting disrupted.

I just knew in my spirit that this cloud was coming for us, and all I could cry in my heart was, "Lord, not today! Not today!" I wasn't ready to let my son go, even though I knew his future was sure if something did happen.

Soon that singular cloud was right outside his window, pelting the building with rain and bursting with thunder. Meanwhile, Chad's breathing was growing more shallow and slow, his lungs filling with fluid. Our family held hands around his bed and prayed, "We release your spirit to the Lord; we release you, Chad." At that instant, the biggest blast of thunder and lightning hit and the building shook. And in the next few moments, Chad breathed his last.

Normally when someone's heart monitor stops blipping and falls into a flatline, my cardiologist's instincts kick in and I go into action. But this wasn't a patient, and this young man wasn't in cardiac arrest; this was my own flesh and blood, and leukemia was doing what the enemy intends: taking my son's life.

I knew that, medically and spiritually speaking, everything had been done for Chad that was humanly possible. And yet we had lost him.

I see-sawed between numbness and anger. A father's numbness and anger. It was as intense as anything I've ever felt, and I barely knew how to contain it.

Deborah and Christian were apparently experiencing far different emotions, because the first words out of my son's mouth were: "Do you feel the peace?" He was secure in the comfort that heaven so often supplies in such situations.

No! I answered to myself. *I don't!*

"I feel it too!" Deb said.

I could hardly believe what I was hearing from them. All I could think was, *God, give me back my son! I just want my son! Please!* But let me be clear: this wasn't the despairing prayer of a man without hope; it was the sorrow of a dad who simply wasn't completely ready to release his child to the Lord. There is a distinct difference.

Jesus felt sadness and wept when His friend Lazarus died. He also vigorously prayed in the Garden of Gethsemane for the cup of crucifixion to pass from Him if there was any other way for God's purposes to be accomplished. So those emotions in the face of death are not ungodly and not a sign that we have lost hope—they are simply marks of our humanity and of life in a fallen world.

Yet in the midst of those honest emotions, Jesus never abandoned His faith in God or His confidence in God's goodness. This is why He was able to ultimately pray, "Not My will, Father, but Yours be done" (see Matt. 26:39) and bear the cross without fear. He wasn't eager to confront death, but He wasn't afraid. He knew that whatever man could do to Him, whatever evil schemes the enemy might employ, He was in His Father's trustworthy hands.

On a far smaller scale, a similar choice fell to me in the minutes after Chad died: I had to decide whether to continue following God with my whole heart, or whether to turn away and go my own way.

I flashed back to the scenes of my life—including the numerous times He had proven His truth and power and His loving presence over the past four years—and I decided to run…to Him. I couldn't fathom His will in that moment; I didn't know why Chad had to die rather than being healed in the here and now, yet I couldn't deny all that the Lord had done or the ironclad credibility of His character. I determined to trust His heart, even though I couldn't make sense of the work of His hand.

For the next hour, Deborah and Christian and I prayed over Chad's body, anointing him again with oil and praying that the Lord would raise him from the dead. But as Chad's face became like soft clay, we knew God's answer was final; our boy was no longer in that earthen shell of a body. He was home. In Paradise.

It was time for us to return to Florida and plan Chad's home-going service.

THE TRUTH OF OUR HOPE

God always delivers and heals His children. But He decides how. And when. If not here on earth, then in heaven.

In the days, months, and years that have followed, we've been sustained by the confidence that God has faithfully delivered our son from his suffering and healed him of his disease. We've been carried forward by a hope that does not die, assured that our temporary loss in this life will be redeemed by a never-ending re-union in heaven. But we've also had moments when we needed encouragement from heaven about the truth that fortifies our hope.

The day after Chad died, Deborah found herself disturbed by memories of what he had endured. Chad's passing had resembled the words of Psalm 18: "The cords of death" surrounded him. The earth trembled. There was thunder and lightning. She was afraid the "torrents of destruction" had "overwhelmed" him, just like they had the psalmist. To a mother's eyes, her son's deathbed was an unnerving scene. *Lord, how can I go the rest of my life thinking of his last breaths where he was struggling so much?* she pleaded.

As Deborah shared her troubled heart with the Lord during her morning prayer time, she heard Him say, "Remember Steven." At first she thought this meant my brother Steven, but as we talked about it, we realized it had to be a reference to the first martyr in the Bible. As that Stephen was being stoned, he looked to heaven and saw Jesus "standing"—not sitting—"at the right hand of God," and he prayed, "Lord Jesus, receive my spirit." Then Scripture says he "fell asleep" (Acts 7:55–60 NKJV).

To be reminded that, as her beloved son passed through the valley of death, Jesus was there to walk him across the threshold of eternity and welcome him home was hugely reassuring. Stephen had endured a martyr's violent murder, yet death was as sleep to him.

This told Deb she didn't have to fear what the evil of cancer had done to Chad's body. Though death had touched our son, its sting couldn't; he'd been held by heaven even while he took his last earthly breaths.

She could say with the apostle Paul: "Death has been swallowed up in victory" (1 Cor. 15:54). Heaven had won, prevailing over earth's suffering and fear. And Chad (whose name means "warrior") had won, his faith and hope fully realized as he opened his eyes in the better realm.

Even now, when our family reads Isaiah 35:3–10 (NLT) our certainty is renewed:

> With this news, strengthen those who have tired hands, and encourage those who have weak knees. Say to those with fearful hearts, "Be strong, and do not fear, for your God is coming to...save you." And when he comes, he will open the eyes of the blind and unplug the ears of the deaf. The lame will leap like a deer, and those who cannot speak will sing for joy! Springs will gush forth in the wilderness, and streams will water the wasteland. The parched ground will become a pool, and springs of water will satisfy the thirsty land...And a great road will go through that once deserted land. It will be named the Highway of Holiness. Evil-minded people will never travel on it...Lions will not lurk along its course, nor any other ferocious beasts. There will be no other dangers. Only the redeemed will walk on it. Those who have been ransomed by the LORD will...enter Jerusalem singing, crowned with everlasting joy. Sorrow and mourning will disappear, and they will be filled with joy and gladness.

When we know that the steadfast God of heaven goes with us, we can walk through the valley of the shadow of death, fearing no evil. We can trust that what seems like an ending to earthly eyes is actually something far better. And therein lies the Christian's faith and hope.

Dan Allender, in a severe wilderness time in his life, once felt the Spirit say to him: "Don't dread any moment that comes from Me." Instead, we need to do as Mike Williams exhorts us: "Take that which is coming against you and use it to lift you higher."

For every child of God—both those who die and those who survive them—death is not what it seems. It is not fatal; it is the next footstep on our path to the gates of heaven and an eternity in God's presence.

Maybe the way to understand this is from a closing scene in Lewis's Chronicles of Narnia. In *The Last Battle*, there is a critical moment when the Pevensie children learn that their supposed dream is something different altogether: "'There was a *real* railway accident,' said Aslan softly. 'Your father and mother and all of you are—as you used to call it in the Shadowlands—dead.'"

Aslan follows this seemingly frightful pronouncement with a faithful one: Yes, "the term is over," he says, but "the holidays have begun. The dream is ended: this is the morning."[5]

Christian faith anchors in this truth: that just past our term on earth is joy. Christian hope, meanwhile, winters in this assurance: that every dark dream gives way to the dawn of God's goodness— and one day, to our first morning of forever.

⌘

I will hope in your name, for your name is good.
Psalm 52:9

The LORD is my light and my salvation; whom shall I fear? The LORD is the stronghold of my life; of whom shall I be afraid?
Psalm 27:1 ESV

Praise be to the God and Father of our Lord Jesus Christ! In his great mercy he has given us new birth into a living hope through the resurrection of Jesus Christ from the dead.

1 Peter 1:3

[Job said to his wife], "Shall we indeed accept good from God and not accept adversity?" In all this Job did not sin with his lips.

Job 2:9–10 NASB

Whether we live or die, we belong to the Lord. For this very reason, Christ died and returned to life so that he might be the Lord of both the dead and the living.

Romans 14:8–9

CHAPTER 13
HEAVEN'S COMFORT

Chad's battle was over. We as a family had fought our fight with everything we had, and while the enemy may have been rejoicing, thinking that cancer had won, we knew the truth: Chad was now in heaven's care—now fully healed. We had prayed the Lord would heal our son, and He had. It was just not in this lifetime.

As Christians, we felt an underlying, persistent peace in knowing Chad was experiencing the glories and perfection of heaven. He was no longer in pain, no longer subject to fear or sadness, no longer held captive by a body that was vulnerable to illness and injury. In this, we took comfort. We still grieved at being separated from him and living without him for the rest of our earthly lives, but we did not mourn "as those who have no hope" (1 Thess. 4:13). Heaven's resurrection power had vanquished the eternal effects of death—and Chad was a beneficiary.

We missed him, though. So deeply. It was an anguish that ran deeper than any physical wound. And we knew our lives would never be the same.

Losing someone you love so much is an amputation. And like all amputations, you can go on with your life . . . but not without making adjustments. For the rest of your days, you travel this earth with a limp and a scar, like Jacob did after his wrestling match with the angel of the Lord. In time you do learn to walk again—but never as easily as you once did.

Our family dynamic was irreversibly changed. The boys had so often functioned as a pair, and now Christian was an only child. Deborah and I had to adjust as parents accordingly.

All these years later, the gap in our family is still there. Yes, we have altered our shape, tried to restructure as a result of that missing piece like an amoeba does. Yet we always feel Chad's absence. Every one of us. Every single day. Christian is grown now, working in ministry, with a wife and two children. But the loss goes with us. And we still need heaven's comfort sometimes.

If we still need it now, we most certainly needed it in the days and months after Chad passed away.

We felt some solace in reflecting on things that happened before his death. For example, for two weeks straight, Chad had dreams of getting out of his wheelchair and running again. I had a dream at that same time, seeing him older and in a white robe.

I know without a doubt that Chad runs unencumbered in his new home. I envision him playing tennis and hiking the hills of Paradise without a shred of struggle, and that makes my heart glad.

It was even easier to picture such a possibility when I heard about one stranger's dream . . .

UNENCUMBERED

During our long stays in Houston at MD Anderson Cancer Center, we frequently attended Joel Osteen's Lakewood Church. Consequently, we got to know some of the staff—these brothers and sisters in the Lord would come and pray with us at the hospital, and certain individuals even committed to praying regularly for our family.

One of those prayer warriors connected with Lakewood was the mother of one of the associate ministers. Just hours before Chad died—on the very day he died—Steve's mom, a woman in her eighties, dreamed she saw Chad sitting on a rocky overlook in the mountains, talking to the Lord. In her dream, Chad was wearing white athletic clothes—*Perhaps the tennis gear he was so fond of?* we thought—and the Lord asked, "Do you want to go back, or come with Me? It's your choice. You can return if you'd like, or you can come home with Me." And in the vision, Chad responded that he wanted to go home with Jesus.

The woman had never met Chad, and she had no idea that Chad was on his deathbed at that exact hour. Only when she called her son that afternoon to tell him what she'd seen—only after she relayed her dream to him—did she learn that Chad had died just that morning.

This was one of many ways that we were comforted by heaven as we journeyed through our grief. Events like these helped us keep our sights on the fact that those who die in Christ do not remain dead. They are separated from us for a time, but they live on, enjoying all the blessings and beyond-abundance of heaven.

First Thessalonians 4:13 states that we don't have to grieve as those without hope because our fellow believers only "sleep in death." Logically speaking, if they sleep in death, it means they awake to life.

Still, because there is so much about heaven that remains a mystery, it's possible to get sucked in by our own shortsightedness, worrying unnecessarily about the status of the departed.

Deborah struggled with this—and many others have too.

ALIVE AND WELL

My wife had the peace of knowing Chad was in heaven—there was no doubt in her mind about where he was—but in retrospect, I think her heart needed assurance about *how* he was. That's the difference between moms and dads sometimes. If we dads know where our kids are, that settles any worries for us. But moms often can't rest until they know their children are actually safe and sound. Maybe this is why the biblical writer actually reminds us: to be "absent from the body" is to be "at home with the Lord" (2 Cor. 5:8 NASB).

Nevertheless, soon after Chad died, Deborah found herself consistently praying, "Father, give me a ray of hope from heaven regarding Chad. Let me know that he's safe with You."

A couple months later, I was invited to speak at the Hunters' church in Texas. They were having a healing service and wanted me to give my testimony about being a doctor.

Deborah didn't go because Christian was still in school, but she had confided to me before I left, "I just need to know that Chad's okay." Honestly, at the time, while I knew such wishes came with the territory of grief, I thought my wife wasn't being very realistic. All I could do was continue to pray that God would comfort her hurting heart.

When I arrived at the Hunters' country church, I was met by a profoundly skinny, very tall, African-American man in a three-piece suit. He may not have been seven feet tall, but he was not much shorter than that.

He greeted me immediately and said, "I'm here to serve you," and started to take my briefcase and books. I told him, "It's okay; I don't have much stuff. You don't have to do that." But he politely insisted, and so I let him carry my briefcase and Bible into the church. We then greeted the ministry team, got settled in, and took seats in the front row on the left side of the sanctuary. My new companion sat there next to me during the entire service, and after I got done speaking, he walked me out to my car.

When I came for the service the next morning, the same thing happened: this tall stranger welcomed me back and said, "I'm here to serve you," and then proceeded to take my Bible and briefcase and escort me to our seats in the front row.

Afterward, he walked me out again, but this time he said, "The Lord wants me to tell you that your son is all right. I see him running and jumping with other children, like a gazelle in a field of tall green grass. I also see him in a crystal-clear river, swimming with the fish and children, and he has such a big smile on his face."

You'd think I would welcome this word, but instead I was

agitated. Who was this guy, and why did he say that? I'd said nothing during the services about losing Chad; I'd only shared about my spiritual journey and some of the healing miracles I'd witnessed.

Unsure what the man's angle was, I found myself almost wondering if this was some cruel game. "Do you know who I am?" I asked. "Do you know anything about me?" Maybe Charles or Frances had told him my story.

"No, sir, I don't," he said calmly.

"What do you know about my son?"

"Nothing. I'm just here to tell you he's okay."

Still trying to figure out what was going on, I continued, "Do you know my family?"

"No."

"Are you sure you don't know my story beyond what I've shared at this church?" I pressed. "Has *anyone* told you about me?"

"Nothing, sir," he gently replied. "I only know that the Lord wants you to know that everything is okay with your son."

I went to dinner that night with the Hunters and a few people from their ministry team, and could hardly wait to find out this guy's story. So shortly after we sat down, I asked, "Who was the tall, dark-skinned man in the front row with me who always wanted to carry my briefcase and Bible?"

They all looked at me with blank faces, and then Frances spoke first. "Chauncey, there was no one in the front row with you."

"Oh yes, there was," I countered. "Both days. The guy was at least six nine or six ten and wore a three-piece suit. You couldn't miss him . . ."

Charles and some of the others chimed in: "Not sure who you're talking about, but we never saw anybody like you're describing." "Seems like we would have noticed him." "Wonder who that could be."

I was dumbstruck. I knew these were men and women of God, and I could tell they weren't joking. Thankfully, they didn't treat me like I was losing my mind either. But I spent the rest of that meal wondering, *How could this be?*

Frances told me later, "It must have been an angel."

That's the only explanation I have. The Bible says that one of the primary roles of angels is to minister to the "sons of earth"—us humans. Evidently God saw fit to minister to my wife through a beanpole of a being, just so she would know that her boy was not only "okay" but free and full of joy. And maybe the fact that the angel tended so specifically to me on that ministry weekend was one way God could demonstrate that I was on heaven's mind too. It's possible I needed the reassurance as much as Deborah did.

I do know that after Chad died, the only thing that gave me peace was doing ministry. When I'd return from ministry trips, my anger and sadness would be gone because I'd seen the glory of the Lord on the mission field.

Mind you, I wasn't angry at God—that had been settled in those minutes at Chad's bed right after he died. I had chosen to devote myself to the Lord rather than believing that He had abandoned me—and that resolve stuck. But I would get dismayed and upset that evil gets even a moment to celebrate.

In those times, God would cloak me in unspeakable peace—the kind that can only come from above; the kind that heaven specializes in.

Deborah fought her grief with worship and the Word and prayer. She would be driving and start to feel the heaviness descend on her, and she would ask the Lord to remove it: "Jesus, I need Your peace." She also kept praise music on—her spiritual garment of praise—and as the words of Scripture were absorbed into her heart and mind, she would experience the otherworldly peace that Jesus promised in John 14:27.

It has now been more than ten years since Chad died, and heaven is still consoling us. Just weeks ago I was treating a woman with heart failure, and she said, "Dr. Crandall, I can see a glow around you, the anointing of God, but there is a small amount of sadness inside you too." Later that same day, a newer patient came to the office looking for me. When we were finally able to talk, he held up a brochure he'd found in the waiting area that shares a little about our family testimony, and with a puzzled look on his face, he asked, "Is that your son?"

"Yes," I answered.

"Well, I need to tell you something," he insisted. "I had this dream last night, and I've never had one like it before. But when I woke up this morning and told my wife and daughter about it, they said, 'You need to tell him.' So here I am.

"This may sound crazy," he continued, "but you were with me, and your son was in the clouds, talking to me, and whatever he said, I was supposed to relay it to you. I'm not sure why you couldn't hear him, but I was telling you everything he spoke. And in the dream your son said, 'Dad, everything's okay, but it's different on this side. There's no pain here. Get Mom and let her know. I want her to know about this too.'"

HEAVEN CAME DOWN

In my finite understanding, I can't tell you what moves heaven to let human beings see past the veil between this world and the next, but I'm grateful for it. Those of us who have suffered loss in the kingdom of earth sometimes need special comfort, an extra touch, from the kingdom of heaven. And when that blessing comes to us, we are motivated to keep trudging faithfully to the finish line of this life.

That happened to Deborah. Late one Sunday evening while driving Christian back to boarding school, she came across a radio program featuring an interview with Randy Alcorn about his new book, *Heaven*. Since it was all based in Scripture, Deborah immediately ordered the book when she got home, and when it arrived, she couldn't put it down.

In one section, she read about the martyrs of the Great Tribulation, assembled in the throne room of God, asking, "When will You avenge our blood?" (see Rev. 6:9–10). Alcorn surmised that the departed saints must be aware of what's happening on earth, but how much, we don't know. This spurred a thought in Deborah, which turned into a prayer: "God, has Chad gone on to live with You now and forgotten about us? Does he still know he has a mom and a dad and a twin brother?"

Not long after this, Deborah, Christian, and I were walking our dogs on the bike trail that runs along the waterfront in West Palm Beach. I went on ahead of my family, trying to get a little workout in. Meanwhile, Deborah was still laboring over this question that the book had prompted. Finally, she turned toward the sky, raised her hands to heaven, and audibly prayed, "O God, is Chad still aware of us down here?"

She says now, "What I was expecting, I didn't know. I just had to ask." But what happened next still amazes us.

As Deborah lowered her arms, she saw—just to her right—three huge letters written in the sky over the water. Christian, who was just a few feet ahead of her, stopped when he heard her prayer, and as he looked out over the water, he exclaimed, "Mom! It says YES!"

"I know," Deborah said expectantly, "but where are the other letters?" Our family had often admired the aerial handiwork of a Christian pilot in our area, and so Deborah assumed he was simply in the middle of another message.

Christian, though, didn't see or hear any plane, and he immediately put two and two together. "There aren't any other letters!" he told her.

"Where's the plane, Christian?" Deborah asked, continuing to scan the skies.

"There isn't a plane! Mom, God heard your prayer! And now it says YES!"

Realizing what had just transpired, the two of them excitedly called out to me, and I ran back to them as quickly as I could. But by the time I got there and was told what happened, the letters had drifted away with the wind.

I was sorry to have missed the skywriting of heaven, but my wife didn't miss the message. This answer to prayer was an enormous relief to her—one she is quick to speak of to this day. I think it left a lasting impression on Christian too.

In times like these, when we've needed specific comfort, both Deborah and I could echo the psalmist: "Whom have I in heaven but you?" (Ps. 73:25).

Christ preached, "Blessed are the poor in spirit, for theirs is the kingdom of heaven. Blessed are those who mourn, for they shall be comforted" (Matt. 5:3–4). It's no surprise that these two "statuses"—the poor in spirit and those who mourn—are positioned together in His beloved Sermon on the Mount. When calamity bursts into your life like shrapnel, you discover pretty quickly what being poor in spirit feels like. Calamity produces suffering and loss, loss that must be mourned.

In his study Bible, Pastor David Jeremiah explains, "Those with destitute hearts [the poor in spirit] sense their spiritual need and seek after God... They have the advantage... of being able to cry out to God for help."[1] Maybe you've never deemed crying out to God for aid or comfort an "advantage," but this is precisely how the kingdom of heaven operates. Things get turned upside down, and its citizens are ministered to in ways that run contrary to earthly ideas of comfort.

Unbelievers think wealth or food and drink or a carefree life are the means to happiness. But it is actually in sharing the sufferings of Christ that we gain the solace and joy we seek. "By his wounds we are healed," says Isaiah 53:5.

RAINING COMFORT

Again and again, our family found consolation in the face of death. And God continues to provide. Sometimes it has come through people being saved or restored to faith by our testimony, or by

Chad's legacy. Sometimes we experience joy and consolation in comforting others with the comfort we've received (2 Cor. 1:3–4). Sometimes the Word of God speaks directly to our pain. And sometimes, it comes through the ongoing work of the Spirit.

He is the divine Comforter appointed by our heavenly Father to guide and go with every believer on this earthly journey. He shines surest, though, in our suffering, giving those who grieve "beauty for ashes, the oil of joy for mourning" (NKJV) and "a garment of praise instead of a spirit of despair" (Isa. 61:3), wherever we are.

During the second cholera epidemic in Haiti in 2010, Deborah and I worked at a cholera camp. I was the only doctor there, and every day I would go from tent to tent and treat every patient. One of the sickest people in this place also became particularly dear to me—an old man I called PaPa. He had cholera, AIDs, and tuberculosis, and he was so dehydrated and ill that he could barely move. Flies were swarming around his head, he was so close to death.

Seeing his struggle, I went over to his cot and said, "Oh, PaPa, I'll pray for you." Then I knelt down on that dirt floor covered in cholera-laced feces, put my hands on his head, and cried out to God for his life. At that moment, the glory of heaven hit: an overwhelming peace and joy so powerful that I wanted to shout it from the treetops.

It was the kingdom of heaven and the comfort of heaven on display.

I often struggle to pierce the darkness of Palm Beach, where people have everything that the kingdom of earth can offer. But on that day, in the poverty and illness of Haiti . . . there was heaven. The Spirit of God came down to comfort, sustain, heal, and make joy a reality on the edge of death.

I said to Deborah, "He even shows up here!" And PaPa lived.

Though you have made me see troubles, many and bitter, you will restore my life again; from the depths of the earth you will again bring me up. You will increase my honor and comfort me once more.

Psalm 71:20–21

Remember your word to your servant, for you have given me hope. My comfort in my suffering is this: Your promise preserves my life.

Psalm 119:49–50

Everything that was written in the past was written to teach us, so that through the endurance taught in the Scriptures and the encouragement they provide we might have hope.

Romans 15:4

Just as we share abundantly in the sufferings of Christ, so also our comfort abounds through Christ.

2 Corinthians 1:5

CHAPTER 14
ALL THINGS NEW

ON EARTH WE live with our past always trailing behind us—often belaboring us—and our future always ahead of us. At some blessed moment, however, the redeemed will find ourselves in God's presence, with the weight of our past removed, and our present and future melded into a glorious, perfect "now" that will never end. In that new heaven on earth, we will be afflicted no more. Filled with jubilation. Wanting nothing. Minus nothing. Missing no one. And without the weight of fear, sin, envy, or strife.

Except for the opportunity of salvation, which is available only on this side of heaven, everything we find on earth will be replaced with a pure and exalted version of itself—from our bodies to our surrounding to our enjoyments—as the Lord makes all things new (Rev. 21:1, 5).

Until that day, we have the kingdom of heaven in our midst, ready to move sky and earth and defeat the forces of evil for this earthly moment. These daily advances foretell the world to come and our victorious future with God.

One of my most vivid views of what will be came through an incident with a longtime patient of mine, Ms. Donna, who was a believer. Most of her life she had worn a special heeled shoe on her right foot because she'd been born with that leg shorter than her left one. By the time I started seeing her as an adult, her right leg was a full *five inches* shorter!

At one visit to my office in her later years, she arrived in a wheelchair; it was just getting too difficult for her to maneuver anymore. I felt such compassion for her. Thankfully, I had just recently learned that Christians can pray in faith for even this condition. So I asked her permission to seek divine restoration for her leg. She looked at me with big eyes but said okay.

I laid hands on her shortened leg and commanded it to grow back to its proper length in the name of Jesus. I continued to hold that short leg and prayed out loud again. Nothing happened. Then I appealed to God silently within my spirit, "Lord, I know You can do this. This woman needs a touch from heaven. Please. Restore her leg in Jesus' mighty name."

When I prayed out loud the third time, the leg started growing right before our eyes. We could even hear her bones adjusting! Ms. Donna screamed, amazed, but in no pain. I watched with joy as God made her leg what it had never, ever been.

Ms. Donna tried to leave my office with her old "elevator shoe" on, but walking with it was no longer possible because that five-inch heel threw her now-equal legs off balance. So what did she do? She walked out barefoot, with words of praise on her lips.

GAINING GROUND

During His tenure on earth, Jesus told His followers to both proclaim and live out this message: "The kingdom of heaven has come near" (Matt. 10:7).

I'm telling you: when the kingdom of heaven is called into our world, all sorts of things happen. Powerful forces are unleashed. The heavens open up, as they did at Jesus' baptism (Mark 1), and the glory of the Most High bursts forth. The prophet Isaiah cried out for this—and we should too: "Oh, that you would rend the heavens and come down, that the mountains might quake at your presence . . . to make Your name known to Your adversaries" (Isa. 64:1–2 NASB)!

When Jesus came to earth, He made it so: healing the sick, delivering the demon-possessed, freeing those who were in emotional or mental bondage. He also commanded His followers to freely travel about and do the same in His name. *The Message* expresses it so poignantly: "Go to the lost, confused people right here in the neighborhood. Tell them that the kingdom is here. Bring health to the sick. Raise the dead. Touch the untouchables. Kick out the demons. You have been treated generously, so live generously" (Matt. 10:7–8).

Every follower of Christ is entitled to do this by His authority. Acts 17:24 says, "The God who made the world and everything in it is the Lord of heaven and earth." Christ doesn't rule only heaven with His Father; He rules heaven *and* earth, including the prince of this earth, Satan. Colossians 1 says Jesus is over all, above all, reigning unconfined. Believers are under His authority today, on earth, as are those who have passed on. This means that whether we suffer "trouble or hardship or persecution or famine or nakedness or danger or sword," we are empowered to be "more than conquerors through him who loved us" (Rom. 8:35, 37).

You've seen it throughout this book: the kingdom of heaven is not separated by space or time. As heaven is dropping down in a Colombian crusade or a miserable hotel room in Togo, it also blankets an evangelistic service in South Dakota. It penetrates the air of earth in a Haitian cholera camp as well as a Florida emergency room.

The kingdom is coming *here*, and *here*, and *here*—all in concert with the great Conductor, Jesus! As we take up our spiritual authority, the situation we're in switches from defeat and darkness and death to victory and light and life. This is the invisible but very real power of the kingdom of heaven.

AN ADVANCING ARMY

Right now, as you read these words, the army of God is advancing. The Word of God is active. The Spirit of God is moving. People are being saved and lives are being transformed. Broken, damaged bodies are being made well. Lost souls are receiving new life. Mental and emotional chains are being released and minds renewed. Hope is being restored. As one life is passing into the presence of God, another life is being birthed somewhere else. It is much like what Ezekiel witnessed in this personal encounter with the Almighty in a valley full of bones:

> The hand of the LORD was on me, and...he said to me, "Prophesy to these bones and say to them, 'Dry bones, hear the word of the LORD!...I will make breath enter you, and you will come to life. I will attach tendons to you and make flesh come upon you and cover you with skin; I will put breath in you, and you will come to life. Then you will know that I am the LORD.'"
>
> So I prophesied as I was commanded. And as I was prophesying, there was a noise, a rattling sound, and the bones came together, bone to bone. I looked, and tendons and flesh appeared on them and skin covered them, but there was no breath in them.
>
> Then he said to me, "Prophesy to the breath; prophesy, son of man, and say to it, 'This is what the Sovereign LORD says: Come, breath, from the four winds and breathe into these slain, that they may live.'" So I prophesied as he commanded me, and breath entered them...
>
> Then he said to me: "Son of man, these bones are the people of Israel. They say, 'Our bones are dried up and our hope is gone; we are cut off.' Therefore prophesy and say to them: 'This is what the Sovereign LORD says: My people, I am going to open your graves and bring you up from them; I will bring you back to the land of Israel. Then you, my people, will

know that I am the LORD...I will put my Spirit in you and you will live, and I will settle you in your own land.' " (Ezekiel 37:1–14)

God does all of this and more for those who turn to Him. He restores dry bones, delivers the distraught, returns the discarded, resettles the wanderers, reconnects the detached, resurrects the dead—and refocuses our sights. And He invites us, His people, to be His hands and feet in that process.

When we take on this blessed task, not only does heaven often ease the burden of those we serve, but our own faith gets refined, just as my accountant's was in the heat and distress of that Haitian cholera camp. Jonathan came as a volunteer; he left a prayer warrior who would carry the light of heaven into other dark corners from that day forward.

The change in him in two weeks' time really struck me on that trip, not just the way the kingdom of heaven healed the sick. Yet I shouldn't have been surprised. This is always the way of God: He moves in our hearts, minds, and lives to make *us* new first, and then graciously enlists us as His partners in setting right what the enemy has corrupted, broken, lied about, taken captive, tried to ruin.

True transformation is a wonderful reality when the kingdom of heaven invades earth. People talk about wanting to change all the time; they pump themselves up with affirming words in hopes of inspiring change; but real renewal happens when the kingdom of light is invited to come and fulfill the King's will on earth, just as it's already done in heaven (Matt. 6:10).

To strive to introduce the kingdom of heaven into the settings and situations of earth is commanded in the Lord's Prayer. As we heed this mandate, we foil the enemy's schemes. People are ministered to. And we, the people of God, gain a heavenly focus.

HEALED FOR SALVATION

Christian Buckley and Ryan Dobson have written: "Our work must always be rooted in the understanding that all of mankind is suffering under both the physical and spiritual consequences of brokenness."[1] With this in view, the gospel of salvation, of sinners being reconciled to Christ, becomes of utmost importance. It is the primary objective of the kingdom of heaven.

I've occasionally had to be reminded of this myself in my passion for seeing people physically healed. I once suggested to a wonderful evangelist in Africa, "Let me set up a tent at your crusades to treat the sick."

He said, "No, rather than treating the sick, we are first going to deliver their souls from hell."

By this, he didn't mean the sick are not a priority. Everywhere in the Bible, the disadvantaged—whether they are poor, infirm, orphaned, or widowed—are a central concern of God's, and were a central concern of Jesus's. This evangelist's statement was rather to affirm that, eternally speaking, salvation is the only way to life. Any earthly healing people receive will not protect them from eternal death and darkness. What will ensure life beyond death, and ultimately their permanent healing in heaven, is the rescue of their souls.

More than once, I've seen the Lord heal bodies so that their souls might be saved. This was true of Jeff Markin, the heart attack victim I shared about who was forty minutes dead and who God brought back to life after I cried out to heaven for his soul.

As Jeff recovered, he and I were able to talk further. He told me of the hellish isolation he felt while we were working to resuscitate him. He reported being thrown into the trash, discarded as if he were nothing—and this experience with the darkness of eternal hopelessness really upset him.

His dismay prompted me to ask if he knew Jesus. Jeff admitted that he knew much *about* Jesus because he'd once been married to a devout Christian. But he had decided to reject Christ back then, and the marriage had dissolved.

I assured him that hell's trash heap is not the destiny for those who call Jesus Lord and Savior, and that as long as we have breath, we can choose differently. After all, God is the God of the living, not just of the dead (Rom. 14:9).

"God must have a call on your life for you to have been brought back from the dead," I reasoned. And he agreed. So I grabbed his hand there in his hospital room, and we prayed together that Jesus would enter his heart and save him.

This was the moment that Jeff's life had been saved for!

Yes, being raised from the dead was a miracle that he and I will both tell for the rest of our lives; it created a media stir at the time and will arouse a certain curiosity for future hearers. But a lot of folks are more interested in God's sensations than in His salvation or companionship. Scripture says that for these who are too blind and deaf to heed the testimony of God's Word, not even someone being brought back to life from the dead will persuade them (Luke 16:31).

The true miracle is the saving of a soul from the clutches of hell. In the supernatural war between the worlds, this registers a far greater defeat to the kingdom of darkness than any physical healing that heaven might perform.

Nonetheless, the kingdom of heaven was marching toward victory and transformation in Jeff's life long before I ever prayed over his lifeless body. Here is the rest of this part of his story.

The night of Jeff's "resurrection" in the ER, I had a meeting with a friend of mine and relayed to him everything that had happened. He called me a few evenings later, incredulous at what he'd just learned: his wife had told Jeff's story to one of her colleagues, and evidently this coworker had fallen to her knees in recognition when she heard the news. The woman said, "That man is my ex-husband! He left our family twenty years ago because I became a Christian and he didn't want that life!"

Turns out, Jeff's ex-wife had been praying for his salvation ever since their split. I also discovered later that Jeff's daughter, when she'd learned her dad had gone to the emergency room, drove to the hospital and was in the parking lot, pleading for his soul while his life was in limbo. "I was born in this hospital, Lord," she prayed. "Please let my father be born again in this same place."

That series of events, as much as any, showed me how God uses His sons and daughters—His earthly ambassadors and warriors— to further His reign in people's lives. Sometimes we go forth in peace, choosing forgiveness instead of bitterness, as Jeff's ex did. Sometimes we go forth and do battle as his daughter did in her parking-lot prayers. Any time, though, that a child of God sees past the human condition to keep a person's eternal condition in mind, God's kingdom comes, and His will is done. Any time a child of God looks past someone else's curses or rejections, rages or jealousies, and seeks the Lord for their healing and salvation, the enemy loses ground and another flag is staked for heaven's sake.

My wife had a similar experience within her own family. Only in their case, the family of the kingdom of heaven joined forces with heaven itself to produce reconciliation and escort a saint home to eternity.

Seven months after her mom went home to be with the Lord, Deborah felt strongly that she had to get to her dad in Birmingham, Alabama. He was staying with her brother, and in his failing health, he'd been heard speaking to a vision of his own deceased mother and brother, "Mama, Clarence, wait; I want to go with you . . ."

When Deborah arrived mid-evening, her brother had just put their dad to bed. However, she sensed the Lord telling her, "You need to reconcile." Her father had been angry that Deborah and I had moved him to Palm Beach at one point, and Deborah had said some things she now regretted. She went to him, took his hand, and told him, "I'm sorry for all the harsh words I said to you."

Her dad forgave her and said he loved her, but he also confessed that he knew he was about to die. Deborah, not wanting to lose another person in her life, urged him to hold on.

All the next day and into the evening, her dad seemed to be in a really deep sleep. By midnight, his breathing was labored. As Deborah read about the glory of the Lord in Solomon's temple, she realized it was time to release her father, so she prayed, "Lord, I long to see your glory in all of this." While sitting by his bedside, she told him, "Daddy, it's okay to go. Take the hands of Jesus and go home."

Moments later, he took his last breath. Then suddenly, in spite of having no vital signs, he slowly raised his hands high in the air, closed his fists like he was grabbing someone's hands, then opened them and lowered his arms. His hands remained in that open position as they rested gently on his lap.

The glory of the Lord was so great in that room, Deborah couldn't stand up; her whole body was shaking. She called me in Haiti to tell me what had happened.

Later she found out that her niece had been in the family's home chapel, interceding for her grandfather on the last night of his life. Madeline was asking the Lord to "take Granddaddy's hands and walk him home." Her nephew Jonathan had a dream that night as well, that Granddaddy was standing before the Lord, and when asked for an accounting of his sins, rather than opening the book of judgment, Jesus said, "I have paid for them."

If you are a believer, and your loved one is in glory, rest in the hope and peace of heaven, for that person has been made well. He or she is free—running, jumping, dancing, whole and healthy.

Now it is your turn; the race is on. And as a member of Team Heaven, you are charged to run with excellence, your eyes focused on the goal: a victorious finish for yourself and for anyone you meet who may not yet be on the path to heaven.

DEATH AS A DOORWAY

The loss of a loved one is often a way that God newly purposes those of us who are left behind.

I like the way songwriter and Christian artist Nichole Nordeman says it in her song "Every Season": "Even now in death You open doors for life to enter."[2]

During Chad's illness, our pastor's wife gave us a one-year Bible. After Chad's funeral, Deborah was even more impassioned spiritually, and she couldn't get enough: "I have to know the Word of God better. I want to know the depths and the mysteries and the secrets that are here, and I will go through this book piece by piece to find them."

Not only has she become one of the most diligent students of the Word I've ever known, but God has used Deborah's spiritual hunger to both further His work on earth and to call forth a redeeming purpose for her life in the face of our enormous loss.

You see, Deborah prayed so hard for our boys before and after their births, and was so absorbed in raising them that, she admits now, she idolized them. In her own words: "All my time centered on them. I was in Bible Study Fellowship, and read the Bible to the boys at night, but I wasn't seeking God like I should or asking Him to control circumstances. I also wasn't aware of spiritual warfare and therefore wasn't asking the Lord to equip our sons with armor. So once Christian was off in boarding school and Chad was in heaven, I found myself asking, 'Lord, what do You want me to do?' And then one day, a woman on the bike trail approached me and asked if we could study the Bible together."

Here's another way the kingdom of heaven reached into my wife's heart. When I prayed to release Chad upon his death, Deborah felt she finally put both of our boys in the hands of the Lord. In the days and years since, all the love she had expended toward them was redirected toward others. Instead of going further inward, she turned outward. And as the Lord expanded her heart and mind, He seeded within her a calling to teach. Now she understands that everyone in her care—whether it's her own flesh and blood or the spiritual children God has bestowed on her—belongs to the Lord and that her job here is to advance His kingdom by raising up young believers.

What's more, she and I have had the opportunity to take part in this renewal together. Not only do we minister at services and events whenever we can, but just this past May, the two of us finally started clearing out Chad's room. The reason? Christian and his wife, Ashley, were expecting their second child, and we were making a place for the baby crib.

My wife and I solemnly removed Chad's jackets, his shirts, his hats, and gently put them away. Not because he has been replaced, but because it was time for this door to be open so that life could enter. As we put away Chad's belongings, I told my wife, "Deb, there's new life here."

Only the kingdom of heaven can make that possible.

When God's kingdom comes to earth, it also frees the captives.

Just a few weeks ago, a woman was in my office crying. She had all kinds of health issues, and a number of spiritual and emotional ones as well. As we talked, I exhorted her, "You're in jail right now—imprisoned by your mind-set and circumstances—but you can be free. Renew your mind. Reprogram it to the things of God. There is a way out. Jesus has the keys to get you out of jail!"

The beauty of the kingdom of heaven is that she can be free, even in her sixties. It doesn't matter whether you're twenty or a hundred and twenty—I've seen patients of all ages delivered of demons, saved by the grace of God for the first time, reconciled with their families, healed of terminal illnesses, relieved of lifelong ailments. I've treated the rich, the drug addicts, the demon-oppressed . . . and their stories of deliverance fill not only this book but could fill a few more!

In all the wondrous possibilities of the kingdom of heaven, everyone can be free. Anyone can be saved. And by heaven's power, absolutely anyone can be changed.

The nastiest man I ever met—and by far the meanest patient I ever treated—was a short Jewish retiree I'll call Jacob Gerber. He made me shake, he was so caustic.

Jacob was always miserable, and he made everybody else miserable too. The way I saw it, he deserved some grace—as a child he'd been imprisoned in a German concentration camp, where he had been experimented on and tortured.

Yet it was all I could do to put up with him.

I had repeatedly told him about God, but he kept refusing. And not in a nice way either.

Nonetheless, the Lord said to me one day, "I want you to pray that I will send you the most difficult patients." So my nurse and I heeded that word that day, asking not just for difficult patients but for tough medical cases. During that time of prayer I felt the Lord assuring me: "I will send them to you so you will see My glory"; I had nothing to fear.

But then, that very evening, the hospital called me away from dinner because Mr. Gerber was headed to the ER with some chest pains. On the way there, I was very frank with God: "I know I prayed to get the most difficult patients, Lord, but I still don't want to talk to this guy. So I'm only going to spend two minutes with him and then turn him over to the doctor on duty."

Of course when I arrived, Jacob was being…Jacob. This time, though, something came over me. I decided I would pray for Jacob rather than be agitated by him.

I'm going to neutralize all the pain I see in this man with the things of God, I determined at the prompting of the Spirit. Then, almost before I knew what I was saying, I announced: "Jacob, you're the most miserable man I've ever met! I don't know what to do with you, but I do know this: the only way you will get better is with Jesus! Will you accept the Lord today?"

You could've heard a feather hit the floor, it was so quiet in that moment.

I don't know which of us was more surprised: Mr. Gerber or me. But in quick succession, he softened and responded, "Yes." And then he wept.

When I cried out to heaven for Jacob, he cried. His wife cried. Heaven came down. The peace of God came down. The love of

Christ came down. He didn't know what had happened; only that he had been touched by a kingdom and a power and a glory not of this world.

I ended up staying there with him for two hours—explaining about the kingdom and the love of God, affirming that his wrongs had been forgiven, assuring that his mind could be relieved of those haunting memories of a wartime era...

Jacob lived a couple years beyond that night, and from that evening forward, he was different. Not only that, but so were his wife and kids. This too is the work of the kingdom of heaven: when one person is changed, everyone and everything connected with them is instantly influenced. Not everyone around them receives the truth, but they are witnesses to it.

The people who knew Jacob saw how different he was, and heaven's glory was evidenced in his transformation. The Lord had declared, "Even the most difficult cases can come to Me." Jesus modeled this while He walked this earth. And now I had seen it with my own two eyes.

Such a change could only originate from one place, one Person: the One who, in evangelist Reinhard Bonnke's words, "stirs hearts, quickens pulses, brings strength and hope."[3] He is the same One who makes all things—all broken things, all seeking hearts, all dry bones—new.

❧

I am the Living One; I was dead, and now look, I am alive for ever and ever! And I hold the keys of death and Hades.

Revelation 1:18

[Jesus said to them:] "If I cast out demons by the Spirit of God, then the kingdom of God has come upon you."

Matthew 12:28 NASB

Now then, we are ambassadors for Christ, as though God were pleading through us: we implore you on Christ's behalf, be reconciled to God.

2 Corinthians 5:20 NKJV

The one whom God has sent speaks the words of God, for God gives the Spirit without limit.

John 3:34

"I have given you authority to trample on snakes and scorpions and to overcome all the power of the enemy; nothing will harm you."

Luke 10:19

CHAPTER 15

ON EARTH AS IN HEAVEN

ALL MY WORK is because of the loss of my son. Both medicine *and* ministry. Because of Chad.

On the day he died, I stood at his bedside and resolved, "I will run to You, God, for the rest of my life." But I also offered up a huge plea to the Lord: "I want a million souls for my son!" Believing that Chad had been martyred by the evil of cancer, I exhorted the Lord to let me see a bounty of souls brought into His kingdom in exchange for my son's life.

This is exactly why I have such a fire inside. I am driven to do everything possible to ready others for the life to come and strengthen them in the life that is.

Medicine can only get them so far; its healing powers expire when we do. But the ministry of heaven makes people whole and sees people home, now and forevermore. So I want to keep pressing in, pursuing God and His purposes even harder.

As Deborah and I travel to the far corners of the world, it's as if we're in the Lord's boat, throwing out a life preserver and praying that people will grab hold. In this phase of our lives, having endured what we have, our priorities are clear: the mission doesn't revolve around us; it's all about rescuing souls and relieving suffering.

That means medicine is no longer my end goal. Being a

cardiologist enables me to do something I love while making a good living. Far more important, it opens up daily opportunities for my second calling, which is to boldly proclaim the gospel and to be Jesus' hands and heart to the lost and hurting.

DON'T BE SURPRISED

Pastor John Hagee has said: "Satan knows that if you survived the pit and head for the palace, you will shake the world." True words. When you persevere through the dark night and start walking in the authority of Christ, don't be surprised if you gain a fresh calling and a further gifting. Jesus' disciples did. And His followers still do. They were commissioned to "go and make disciples of all nations" (Matt. 28:19). And He fortified their courage with the promise that, in His name, they would drive out demons, speak in new tongues, pick up snakes with their hands, and make the sick well (Mark 16:17–20).

For me, the way the Spirit moved whenever I would pray over people or preach during ministry trips showed me that the Lord had indeed empowered me in this new calling. It was a spiritual gifting affirmed by the evangelists and missionaries I served under as well. For example, the night before she died, Frances Hunter called to leave me with these words: "Chauncey, you must take your story to the nations."

And then there was one nighttime vision...

I dreamed the Lord and I were in the mountains together when I glimpsed a distant, flickering light like a campfire.

"Do you see that?" He asked. "Many ministers run for that fire, but they never reach it. It is always at a distance. I haven't placed you away from the fire; I've put you in the middle of it. Honor Me with it."

I still strive to hone my surgical skills and give every patient my best medical skills. The difference is that now, no matter where I am—whether it's a medical setting or not—I'm attuned to how much bigger the kingdom's work is, and that it is *all* the work of the Lord: tending to the sick, proclaiming good news to the poor, binding up the brokenhearted, proclaiming "freedom for the captives and release from darkness for the prisoners" (Isa. 61:1). I also understand as never before that to fulfill my calling, I need the fullness of the kingdom. To properly tend to the whole person and not just their bodily health, I need all the Word I can read; all the Scripture I can memorize; all the praise I can offer; every prayer I can utter; the whole armor of God; and more and more of the Spirit of God moving in me.

In every way, I'm just like you. You encounter people every day who need healing. Some of them need physical or practical care; many, many more need spiritual care. In either condition, are we just going to let the sickness go on? Or will we step up and serve, laying on hands and calling down the kingdom of heaven and victory in Jesus' name?

KINGDOM ADVANCING

An important kingdom principle—and one of the best means to ministry—is to look beyond the surface of a person's condition. Sometimes what seems a physical ailment is actually rooted in a spiritual cause. If you relieve the spiritual disease, the physical symptoms immediately improve.

Not long ago a patient of mine, a divorced father who was visiting my office, shared with me his concern about his teenage daughter, who had just been diagnosed with severe depression. The girl—a very bright, gifted student—was cutting herself and plagued by thoughts of suicide. Nothing the doctors tried was working—no medication, no counseling. I also learned the girl's mother had battled a chronic illness, though she was currently in remission.

Based on all the details my patient shared, I was convinced the daughter was loaded with demons and that the spirit of death was on her, and I told the man so. This patient is a believer, but admitted he knew little of how to deal with demons and spirits. Yet he was committed to doing anything to save his daughter.

I advised this father to go to the girl immediately and pray over her, because it seemed death was knocking. I also taught my patient how to pray over someone and cast out any oppressive spirits.

The dad traveled to New York to see his daughter two days later. The next time he visited my office, he excitedly reported: "It worked! My daughter is back in school, in her right mind; no cutting, no depression, no suicidal thoughts!"

We rejoiced together, reminded once more that, as Christians, we carry the kingdom of heaven with us. It is in us, operating through us, at any and all times. All we must do is call it down in Jesus' mighty name.

I've said this before in these pages, but please don't miss it: Any one of us who walks in faith and obedience is not only allowed but commanded to call heaven down, as Jesus did in the Lord's Prayer. Why? Because God wants everything to "be . . . on earth as it is in heaven" (Matt. 6:10).

God is set on restoring His righteous kingdom. He is orchestrating world events at this very moment to bring this to pass on an apocalyptic level one day. Then, the kingdom of darkness will be put away and all that remains will be made new. Until that future hour, we need to be advancing the kingdom of heaven and taking the promised land. Reclaiming lost territory. Rebuilding what the enemy has destroyed.

TIME TO WORK

In the days of Haggai the prophet, only a fraction of the remnant who returned to Jerusalem after their captivity in Babylon were old enough to remember the former glory of the Lord's temple. The ruins they returned to were enough to dishearten even the heartiest of the older generation, for this house of worship—this wondrous place of crafted cedar and gold and woven fabric and jewels that

God's glory had inhabited—now seemed to them "like nothing" (Hag. 2:3).

But the prophecy delivered to the leadership and citizens of Israel was this:

"Now be strong, Zerubbabel [governor of Judah]...Be strong, Joshua...the high priest. Be strong, all you people of the land...and work. For I am with you," declares the LORD Almighty... "And my Spirit remains among you. Do not fear...In a little while I will once more shake the heavens and the earth, the sea and the dry land. I will shake all nations...and I will fill this house with glory...The glory of this present house will be greater than the glory of the former house," says the LORD Almighty. "And in this place I will grant peace." (Haggai 2:4–7, 9)

For now, we are "the temple of the living God" (2 Cor. 6:16). God is in the process of reclamation; we are His "coworkers" (2 Cor. 6:1), and He bids His people to work. Sometimes this means we assume our battle positions and fight the enemy head-on as soldiers of the King. Always, it means we love and extend peace to those whom the world would cast aside as ambassadors of a heavenly kingdom.

There are times I'm praying for someone and an overwhelming, almost inexplicable love for that person will wash over me. The Lord showers me with love, and I pray it forward. Paul spoke of this in his letter to the Christians in Colossae: "We have heard of your faith in Christ Jesus and of the love you have for all God's people—the faith and love that spring from the hope stored up for you in heaven...In the same way, the gospel is bearing fruit and growing throughout the whole world—just as it has been doing among you since the day you heard it and truly understood God's grace" (Col. 1:4–6).

That the gospel would advance on earth through love *and*

power makes a lot of sense, since these are foundational attributes of heaven. The heavenly kingdom is one of love and light, not just holiness and might. We are warriors of the light, partnering with King Jesus to bring His realm into this one.

How do we do this?

Before Jesus ascended to heaven to prepare it for our arrival (John 14:2–3), He and God the Father made sure we were equipped with everything we would need to continue heaven's work in the now while we wait for the "not yet" to come. We carry more than just Jesus' example with us; we go forward with:

- Jesus interceding for us at the right hand of God (Romans 8:34).
- The Advocate, the Holy Spirit, teaching us all things and reminding us of everything Jesus said (John 14:26).
- The peace of Christ (John 14:27).
- The gospel message, which is "the power of God that brings salvation to everyone who believes" (Rom. 1:16).
- The living, penetrating, convicting word of God (Heb. 4:12).

What amazes me is this parting assurance from Jesus: "Very truly I tell you, whoever believes in me will do the works I have been doing, and they will do *even greater things than these*... You may ask me for anything in my name, and I will do it" (John 14:12–14)! The One who healed lepers, fed five thousand with a few loaves and fishes, and made the lame to walk promised His followers that their work on earth would exceed His!

Sure enough, when the seventy disciples—Jesus' advance teams—returned from their first ministry trips, they were astounded: "Lord, even the demons submit to us in your name." Yet Christ articulated a greater priority, so they would keep their eyes on the goal: "Do not rejoice that the spirits submit to you, but rejoice that your names are written in heaven." (Luke 10:17–20).

This is the charge to everyone who goes into all the world in His name. Casting out demons and curing infirmities are the "main event" by earth's accounts. But heaven knows the score. There is no miracle more priceless than that of a soul delivered from everlasting death.

ON MISSION

You know what happened to the dry bones in the valley when Ezekiel prophesied for the Lord to breathe life into them? "They came to life and stood up on their feet—a vast army" (Ezek. 37:10).

At some point, the enemy has attacked every one of us and left us for dead in life's valley. Yet for all those who have been rescued and resurrected from the decay of death, we are on a reconnaissance mission to make sure no one gets left behind.

Among our marching orders are these:

- "When you enter a town and are welcomed...heal the sick who are there and tell them, 'The kingdom of God has come near to you.'" (Luke 10:8–9)
- "If you love Me, keep My commands" (John 14:15).
- "Seek first His kingdom and His righteousness" (Matt. 6:33).
- "Set your minds on things above, not on earthly things" (Col. 3:2).
- "Put on the full armor of God, so that you can take your stand against the devil's schemes...Stand firm then, with the belt of truth buckled around your waist, with the breastplate of righteousness in place, and with your feet fitted with the readiness that comes from the gospel of peace. In addition to all this, take up the shield of faith, with which you can extinguish all the flaming arrows of the evil one. Take the helmet of salvation and the sword of the Spirit, which is the word of God" (Eph. 6:11, 14–17).
- "Pray in the Spirit on all occasions with all kinds of prayers and requests...Be alert and always keep on praying for all the Lord's people" (Eph. 6:18).

In other words, we are commanded to take up our weapons and

fight! Thankfully, "the weapons we fight with are not the weapons of the world. On the contrary, they have divine power to demolish strongholds" (2 Cor. 10:4).

When we do as our Commander in Chief says, we gain daily victories for His kingdom. We are then in position to help our comrades triumph as well. And together, the entire army of God on earth marches forward so that those who are without God and without hope can know the ultimate victory: heaven.

The kingdom of heaven is one of conquest, not defeat. But as with any battle, we must prepare ourselves. This means, first and foremost, diligently pursuing God and the things above. This is the heart of our earthly mission.

I can't emphasize enough the seriousness of our vertical pursuit of God if we want to fulfill our commission. Our society, even many of our churches, wants to focus on horizontal pursuits—such as increased social services—as the solution to people's ills. Yet God has established His church, His people, His army to carry out the priorities of His eternal kingdom.

It's really not enough to give your heart to Christ, however. What sets apart the warriors from the enlisted ranks is giving the Lord your *life*. Are you "all in" with God? Is eternity always in your sights? Do you heed the Spirit and know the Word so that your choices align with the kingdom's objectives? Are you refusing to live any lies? Are you faithful in your relationships, pure and un-compromised in all your ways? Is your money surrendered to God and appointed for His purposes? Is your time?

If so, then fight toward the finish line—and keep fighting—for the kingdom of God has arrived! Through you, the peace and victory of heaven can come over your children, your marriage, your neighborhood and business. "This is the heritage of the servants of the Lord," wrote the prophet Isaiah. "No weapon formed against you shall prosper, and every tongue which rises against you in judgment you shall condemn [silence]" (Isa. 54:17 NKJV).

FIGHT TO WIN

I always want to stay on the narrow path so I can grab the cloak of the Lord and see what He is doing, and then go forth in His sustaining power. Completing His work is my utmost concern. To do it, I have to fight to win. And fighting to win requires studying up on the enemy so I can vigilantly fend off his schemes.

Satan won't take just one tack and give up if it doesn't succeed; he will keep warring against us, using different methods. So expect it! Train yourself in the Word and the movements of the Spirit before the day of evil comes. Arm yourself with praise and prayer and fasting and meditation in the Scriptures. Exercise your faith muscles daily. And above all, be ready to adjust your approach as the situation demands.

In my profession, I've noticed that doctors who are trained in only one university system tend to be less adaptable than those who have trained in multiple systems. Spiritually, we need to take a lesson from this and do battle from different angles.

The win is won by various means. As the people of God—as His ambassadors and army in this world—we have to know how to adapt to achieve victory, being prepared to use multiple strategies. The enemy employs varying tactics all the time, so why shouldn't we?

During one of the cholera outbreaks that I worked in Haiti, a medical team from one of America's most prestigious universities didn't know how to function because they were without their usual supplies and nothing fit their protocol. Consequently, their quality of care for these earthquake victims fell far short of what they were used to giving their patients back home.

The missionary doctors, on the other hand, thrived. These men and women who have little to no resources for treating the sick on a day-to-day basis somehow found a way and were able to save multiple lives because they'd learned to adjust to unexpected conditions. When you have nothing, you learn to make do and make an impact anyway.

If these doctors could excel while face-to-face with catastrophic circumstances, there should be no stopping us, for we have the supernatural power of heaven and the infinite wisdom of the Holy Spirit guiding us. We also have the Word of God, our primary weapon. His Word carries such great power that it will change people. I don't have to, and you don't have to; God will. Our role is to minister and proclaim the Word. Heaven will do the rest.

Spiritual adaptability never leaves us without hope, and it never leaves us in futility like my Ivy League colleagues. There is always something that can be done.

I try to have the Word with me at all times—in my memory, for sure, but also keeping a small Bible close by. Speaking aloud the Word will instill peace and confound the enemy. Likewise, the name of Jesus forces demons to flee.

The truth of the Word for the situation alters our surrounding environment. Instantly. By heaven's power we can transform an entire room—any room we enter—turning it into a place of triumph.

Praise music is another way to wage battle. So is prayer, and verbally rebuking evil spirits, and gathering together with other Christians for worship and intercession. And always, the Holy Spirit will prompt you in what to do and say. Trust Him, even if it doesn't quite seem rational. Because in the kingdom of heaven, things are different.

In this kingdom...

Life prevails over death.
Mourning is dispelled with a song of praise.
Hope shines in the deepest dark.
Those who hunger and thirst grow full.
Earth's setbacks and losses actually advance the gospel.
And the poor in spirit are blessed.

How do I know? Because I've reached for heaven, and heaven

has reached back for me. I've stood my spiritual ground in "the day of evil," and after everything, I still stand (Eph. 6:13). I've cried out to heaven on behalf of my patients and my loved ones, and its love and goodness and joy and peace have washed over us. In a jungle church, inside a cholera tent, in a surgical theater at a metropolitan hospital, at my teenager's deathbed, on the pages of the sky over Palm Beach—and most of all, in the hearts and minds of those I love and care for.

As long as we walk this earthly sod, heaven's business is ours. We must be about serving the disadvantaged, relieving the sick, and saving the lost. We must strive to tell people that the Lord is real and heaven *is*. That we have reliable hope. And that even when immersed in loss, all is well.

One day, when I turn toward home, heaven will be awaiting me with open arms. For now, it is here with me, here among us—our firepower as we fight the good fight till His kingdom, His eternal kingdom, comes.

❧

[The Spirit of truth] lives with you and will be in you . . . Because I live, you also will live . . . You will realize that I am in my Father, and you are in me, and I am in you.

John 14:17, 19–20

If God is for us, who can be against us?

Romans 8:31

Since we are surrounded by such a great cloud of witnesses, let us throw off everything that hinders and the sin that so easily entangles. And let us run with perseverance the race marked out for us, fixing our eyes on Jesus, the pioneer and perfecter of faith. For the joy set before him he endured the cross, scorning its shame, and sat down at the right hand of the throne of God. Consider him who endured such opposition from sinners, so that you will not grow weary and lose heart.

Hebrews 12:1–3

Do you not know that in a race all the runners run, but only one gets the prize? Run in such a way as to get the prize. Everyone who competes in the games goes into strict training. They do it to get a crown that will not last, but we do it to get a crown that will last forever.

1 Corinthians 9:24–25

THE KINGDOM IS NEAR

I USED TO think my purpose was to treat the sick. After everything that has happened, I've learned my purpose is to treat the sick *and* the lost. To discern through the Holy Spirit what ails them—whether it's a physical problem or a prevailing sin or spiritual bondage or demonic oppression—and remedy it as best I can with the instruments of the kingdom of heaven. I can't fix anyone's sin or bondage, but I know Who will, and so I always want to point people to the Great Physician, Jesus Christ. That is my greatest joy.

I especially love working in Third World hospitals that no one else wants to visit. Those doctors have nothing from a worldly perspective, and all I have is Jesus. Yet we march together to treat the sick. And along the way, I get to proclaim Christ as Deliverer and Savior, harvesting souls and promoting healing by the power of God.

In this book I've shared about some of the battles I've been thrust into in the spiritual realm—battles I've seen vividly played out here on earth. I've also tried to arm you with the assurance God has given me: that because of the truth of eternity, we can speak light into the darkness and life into death. Earth is not the end, life doesn't stop here, and death does not have to have the last word.

I hope that you've been awakened to all of this in these pages, because my desire is for us to join together in the battle for the heart. Yes, I'm the heart doctor; I fight death every day in my work. But I am also a "tender of the heart," spiritually speaking—someone who passionately longs for souls to be saved so they may escape the eternal emptiness and agony of hell—and my most important work is daily professing healing and life over my patients. This is the ministry we all share in. In Jeremiah 15:19 the Lord told His servant, "If you utter worthy . . . words, you will be my spokesman." I'm no Jeremiah, and you probably don't profess to be either. Yet by relying on God and learning to properly handle His Word, our words and actions can be worthy of God's calling in every place He puts us, among every person He puts us with.

I always wanted to help people. Since childhood, that was my longing. Now I get to live it in full—spiritually, not just professionally—where the whole of my life is to "press on to that other country and to help others to do the same" (C. S. Lewis, *Mere Christianity*). And as I've sought to do God's work, He continues to give me ever more work to do.

The Lord recently told me, "Go in and give them the victory." This only deepened my resolve to tell my patients, and anyone else who will listen, about heaven. Along with that resolve, I am believing God for those million souls for my son Chad. Day by day, one by one, it is happening.

All that matters is getting people to the finish line of their lives so they can be forever in God's presence. This demands not only that I testify about what I've seen and heard of heaven's truths but that I run my race with endurance—increasing in faith, persistent in hope, bold in belief. I want to be an "oak of righteousness," as the ancient prophet declared, "a planting of the LORD for the display of his splendor" (Isa. 61:3).

God has been so faithful. Through the tragedies of earth and the tales of heaven I've shared with you here, my own trust has been restored. The stakes of my faith are firmly established, and I am more convinced than ever that the next world is more real than this one. Jesus has prepared it for us, and any views of it that we are given from here are meant to transform our beliefs and our choices, making life new. I hope this has happened for you as you've read.

If it hasn't yet, take these words from Romans 10 to heart, for the kingdom of heaven is near you. The word of faith is in your mouth and heart, and it can be yours with one decision, one plea: "If you confess with your mouth, Jesus is Lord, and believe in your heart that God raised him from the dead, you will be saved" (vv. 8–9).

Scripture says, "Anyone who trusts in him will never be put to shame" (v. 11). Believe it. Claim it. Cry out to heaven, for "everyone who calls on the name of the Lord will be saved" (v. 13).

A PRAYER FOR SALVATION

If you do not have a relationship with the Lord today, I would like to reach out to you and pray with you that you would come to Jesus and enter the kingdom of God. "Now is the favorable time; behold, now is the day of salvation" (2 Cor. 6:20 ESV)!

Just say this simple prayer:

Dear Lord Jesus, I come to You now.
Forgive me of my sins. Enter my heart, Lord Jesus.
I confess You as my Lord and my Savior.
Thank You, Jesus; I love You forever.

If you prayed this prayer, you are now walking with the King of kings and the Lord of lords; your eternal life has just begun!

I will be praying for you in Jesus' mighty name.

Chauncey W. Crandall IV, MD

TO CONTACT ME, WRITE TO:

Chauncey Crandall, MD
c/o The Chadwick Foundation
P.O. Box 3046
Palm Beach, Florida 33480

Or you can reach me online at: chaunceycrandall.com

NOTES

CHAPTER 2: LOOK TO THE LIGHT

1 C. S. Lewis, *Surprised by Joy: The Shape of My Early Life* (New York: Harcourt, Brace, Jovanovich, 1955), 177.

CHAPTER 3: LOSING MY RELIGION

1 C. S. Lewis, *The Screwtape Letters*, Revised Edition (New York: Macmillan, 1961), 11-12.

CHAPTER 5: PRACTICING HEAVEN'S PRESENCE

1 Reinhard Bonnke, posted on Facebook.com/ evangelistreinhardbonnke, October 15, 2014.

CHAPTER 6: FIRE FROM HEAVEN

1 Reinhard Bonnke, posted on Facebook.com/ evangelistreinhardbonnke, October 18, 2014.

2 Charles and Frances Hunter, *How to Heal the Sick* (New Kensington, PA: Whitaker, 2000).

CHAPTER 7: TWO KINGDOMS

1 John R. Kohlenberger III, gen. ed., *NIV Nave's Topical Bible* (Grand Rapids, MI: Zondervan, 1992), "Ben Hinnom."

CHAPTER 8: RESURRECTION POWER

1 Merold Westphal, "Review of Van A. Harvey *The Historian and the Believer*," quoted in Josh McDowell, *A Ready Defense: The Best of Josh McDowell*, comp. Bill Wilson (San Bernardino, CA: Here's Life, 1990), 124.

2 Josh McDowell, *A Ready Defense*, 125.

CHAPTER 9: THE *REAL* REAL WORLD

1 C. S. Lewis, *Mere Christianity* Book III (New York: Macmillan, 1952), 120.

2 Mother Teresa, *Mother Teresa: A Simple Path*, comp. Lucinda Vardey (New York: Ballantine, 1995), 73.

3 Sarah Young, *Dear Jesus: Seeking His Life in Your Life* (Nashville, TN: Thomas Nelson, 2007), 94.

4 C. S. Lewis, *The Weight of Glory* (San Francisco: HarperOne, 2001), 45.

5 Charles Spurgeon, "Though He Were Dead." Sermon at the Metropolitan Tabernacle, Newington, September 14, 1884. spurgeon.org/sermons/1799.htm.

6 Erwin W. Lutzer, *One Minute After You Die: A Preview of Your Final Destination* (Chicago: Moody, 1997), 9.

7 Portions of the material from this section are adapted from Norman L. Geisler and Ronald M. Brooks, *When Skeptics Ask: A Handbook of Christian Evidences*, 8th ed. (Grand Rapids, MI: Baker, 2003), 118-127, and Josh McDowell, *A Ready Defense*, 216-240.

8 Geisler and Brooks, *When Skeptics Ask*, 118.

9   McDowell, *A Ready Defense*, 236-237.

10 John Hagee, *The Three Heavens: Angels, Demons and What Lies Ahead* (Brentwood, TN: Worthy, 2015).

11 Zac Maloy, Luke Laird, and Carrie Underwood, "Temporary Home" (Sony/ATV Music Publishing, LLC; Universal Music Publishing Group). Find the song on her *Play On* album (Arista Nashville, 2009).

12 Lutzer, *One Minute After You Die*, 11-12.

13 Jeremy Binns, "We will walk on streets of gold" blog, jeremybinns.com, posted November 16, 2013.

14 C. T. Studd (1860-1931), "Only One Life, 'Twill Soon Be Past." Public domain.

15 Warren Wiersbe, *The Wiersbe Bible Commentary: New Testament* (Colorado Springs, CO: David C. Cook, 2007), 514.

16 Ted Dekker, *The Slumber of Christianity: Awakening a Passion for Heaven on Earth* (Nashville, TN: Thomas Nelson, 2005), 95-96.

17 Steve Berger, *Between Heaven and Earth: Finding Hope, Courage, and Passion Through a Fresh Vision of Heaven* (Bloomington, MN: Bethany House, 2014), eBook.

CHAPTER 10: A PLACE LIKE NO OTHER

1   Hagee, *The Three Heavens*, 266.

2   Randy Alcorn, *Heaven* (Carol Stream, IL: Tyndale, 2004), 259.

3   For example, Dr. David Jeremiah. See his note on Hebrews 12:1 in *The Jeremiah Study Bible* (Brentwood, TN: Worthy, 2013).

4   John R. Rice, *Bible Facts About Heaven: Sweet Home of the Departed Saints* (Murfreesboro, TN: Sword of the Lord, 1940), eBook.

5   J. Sidlow Baxter, *The Other Side of Death: What the Bible Teaches about Heaven and Hell* (Grand Rapids, MI: Kregel, 1997), 61.

6   C. S. Lewis, *The Last Battle,* The Chronicles of Narnia (New York: HarperCollins, 1956, 1984), 195.

7   Keith A. Butler, *Hell: You Don't Want to Go There* (Word of Faith Ministries, 2000).

8   Lewis, *The Last Battle*, 196.

9   John F. MacArthur, *The Glory of Heaven* (Wheaton, IL: Crossway, 1996), 109.

10   Ibid., 107.

11   Steven J. Lawson, *Heaven Help Us!* (Colorado Springs, CO: NavPress, 1995), 128.

12   Some material in this section was adapted from Steve Berger, *Between Heaven and Earth,* and various contributors to Randy Alcorn, *Eternal Perspectives: A Collection of Quotations on Heaven, the New Earth, and Life After Death* (Carol Stream, IL: Tyndale, 2012).

13   William Hendriksen, *More Than Conquerors* (Grand Rapids, MI: Baker, 1961), 249.

14   Jonathan Edwards, quoted in Dustin W. Benge, *A Journey Toward Heaven: Daily Devotions from the Sermons of Jonathan Edwards* (Grand Rapids, MI: Reformation Heritage, 2012), 8.

15   Joni Eareckson Tada, *Heaven: Your Real Home* (Grand Rapids, MI: Zondervan, 1995), 83–84.

CHAPTER 11: FOREVER CHANGED

1   Richard Baxter, *The Saints' Everlasting Rest*, abr. Benjamin Fawcett, 6th ed. (Glasgow: William Collins, 1831), eBook.

2   Tada, *Heaven*, 39.

3   Jill Briscoe, *Heaven and Hell* (Wheaton, IL: Victor, 1990), 35–36.

4   Hank Hanegraaff, *The Complete Bible Answer Book,* Collector's Edition (Nashville, TN: Thomas Nelson, 2008), 451.

5   Ibid., 453.

6   Ibid., 454.

7   Captain Dale Black with Ken Gire, *Flight to Heaven: A Plane Crash . . . a Lone Survivor . . . a Journey to Heaven—and Back* (Bloomington, MN: Bethany House, 2010), 109.

8   C. H. Spurgeon, *The Treasury of David* (Peabody, MA: Hendrickson, 1988), 212.

9   Dwight L. Moody, *Heaven: How to Get There*, Cosimo Classics (New York: Cosimo, 2005), 52.

10   Herbert Lockyer, *All the Promises of the Bible* (Grand Rapids, MI: Zondervan, 1962), 314.

11   Randy Alcorn, *TouchPoints: Heaven* (Carol Stream, IL: Tyndale, 2006), 113–114.

12   Lutzer, *One Minute After You Die*, 63–67.

13   Mark Buchanan, *Things Unseen* (Sisters, OR: Multnomah, 2002), 76.

14   Alcorn, *Heaven*, 400–401.

15   E. M. Bounds, *Heaven: A Place, a City, a Home* (London: Elephants, Ltd. and Fleming H. Revell, 1921), 145.

16   David Jeremiah, "The New Jerusalem" article (Revelation 21:1–2), *The Jeremiah Study Bible*.

CHAPTER 12: A LIVING HOPE

1   C. S. Lewis, *A Grief Observed* (London: Faber and Faber, 1961), 20–21.

2   Hanegraaff, *The Complete Bible Answer Book,* Collector's Edition, 33.

3   Martin Luther, *Galatians*, The Crossway Classic Commentaries, ed. Alister McGrath and J. I. Packer (Wheaton, IL: Crossway, 1998), 250–251.

4   Dan B. Allender, PhD, *The Healing Path: How the Hurts in Your Past Can Lead You to a More Abundant Life* (Colorado Springs, CO: Waterbrook, 1999), 22.

5   Lewis, *The Last Battle*, 210.

CHAPTER 13: HEAVEN'S COMFORT

1   David Jeremiah, "Happiness According to Jesus" sidebar (Matthew 5:1–12), *The Jeremiah Study Bible*.

CHAPTER 14: ALL THINGS NEW

1   Christian Buckley and Ryan Dobson, *Humanitarian Jesus: Social Justice and the Cross* (Chicago: Moody, 2010), 66.

2   Nichole Nordeman, "Every Season," from the Sparrow

Records album *This Mystery* (Ariose Music, admin. by EMI CMG Publishing, 2000).

3   Reinhard Bonnke, posted on Facebook.com/ evangelistreinhardbonnke, October 13, 2014.

ACKNOWLEDGMENTS

Many people have been influential in helping me understand the realities of heaven and the truths of the kingdom. To my patients and colleagues, as well as the missionaries and evangelists and pastors who have allowed me to join them in their work, thank you— you've helped me see the unseen and focus on what really matters.

I particularly want to thank Reinhard Bonnke, David Hogan, Greg Rider, Andrew McMillan, Larry and Joel Stockstill, and the late Charles and Frances Hunter for their eternal investment in me personally and in my spiritual training. Your dedication to the salvation and healing of souls around the world has transformed the way I approach the lost and hurting, and I will never be the same.

I also want to thank my beautiful wife, Deborah, who has walked every step of this journey with me. You have loved and prayed me through it all, and I cherish you for it. No one has a better partner in life and ministry than the one I have in you.

I'm also thankful for our son Christian, who has been such a gift to our lives. You were a warrior for your twin brother during his illness; you have since become a man of God, and I am immensely proud of you. I consider myself blessed beyond measure with this family of mine.

Where this book is concerned, I first want to thank my agent, Sealy Yates. You have been a friend and an advocate from day one, and I am grateful for everything you have done to help me get this message into the hands of people I would never have met otherwise. Likewise, I deeply appreciate Joey Paul at FaithWords for his instantaneous support of and belief in this work. There are other books on heaven, but you recognized the uniqueness of mine. Thank you as well to Rolf Zettersten and the entire FaithWords team for allowing this doctor to publish with you again. I pray the Lord uses our efforts to advance His kingdom and reap a harvest of souls. Additionally, I want to thank Kris Bearss for pouring her heart and talents into this project. She understood from the start Who this book was about and why, and she carried that charge with her onto the finished page. It has been my privilege to have worked with a collaborator who not only loves the Lord but who loves His Word. May God anoint your service to Him and your work with the tribe He has given you. It is all for His glory.

And last but not least, I owe my every heartbeat to my Creator and Lord, the God of heaven and earth. Thank You for saving me, for supplying me in every ordeal and battle, and for sending me into the fields where You're working. As long as I have breath, or until Your kingdom comes, Lord, I will join You in the harvest of souls until Your will is done, on earth as it is in heaven.

SCRIPTURE PERMISSIONS